THE AUTOBIOGRAPHY OF
SAINT MARGARET MARY

THE AUTOBIOGRAPHY OF

SAINT MARGARET MARY

Newly translated from the French
with an introduction by

Vincent Kerns
Missionary of St Francis de Sales

THE NEWMAN PRESS
WESTMINSTER, MD

DARTON, LONGMAN & TODD
LONDON

DARTON, LONGMAN & TODD LTD
29a Gloucester Road,
London, SW7

THE NEWMAN PRESS
Westminster, Md

PRINTED IN GREAT BRITAIN BY NORTHUMBERLAND PRESS
LIMITED GATESHEAD ON TYNE. EX PARTE CONGREGA-
TIONIS: NIHIL OBSTAT JOSEPH DAVIS, M.S.F.S., S.T.L.
IMPRIMI POTEST: FRANCISCUS L. HAMILTON, M.S.F.S.
SUPERIOR REGIONALIS ANGLIAE. NIHIL OBSTAT CAROLUS
DAVIS, S.T.L., CENSOR DEPUTATUS. IMPRIMATUR E.
MORROGH BERNARD, VIC. GEN., WESTMONASTERII, DIE
22A OCTOBRIS, 1960. THE NIHIL OBSTAT AND IMPRIMATUR
ARE A DECLARATION THAT A BOOK OR PAMPHLET IS CON-
SIDERED TO BE FREE FROM DOCTRINAL OR MORAL ERROR.
IT IS NOT IMPLIED THAT THOSE WHO HAVE GRANTED
THE NIHIL OBSTAT AND IMPRIMATUR AGREE WITH THE
CONTENTS, OPINIONS OR STATEMENTS EXPRESSED

Lord Jesus Christ,
who didst wondrously reveal
the inscrutable treasures of thy heart
to the blessed maiden Margaret Mary,
through her merits and example
give us grace to love thee
above all and in all things,
so that we may deserve to have in that same
heart of thine
our everlasting abode.

FOR MY MOTHER

CONTENTS

CONTENTS

INTRODUCTION

S T FRANCIS DE SALES has an honoured place in the history of devotion to the Sacred Heart. He was the founder of the Visitation nuns, an Order to which he gave a special spirit in their Constitutions—a spirit which was to set in relief the later revelations of the Sacred Heart to St Margaret Mary.

On 10 June 1611, St Francis wrote to St Jane Frances de Chantal: 'I thought, if you agree, that we ought to take as armorial bearings a single heart pierced by two arrows, and set in a crown of thorns. This plain heart could form the base of a cross inscribed with the sacred names of Jesus and Mary. . . . For truly, our little Congregation is the work of the hearts of Jesus and Mary. By opening his sacred Heart, the dying Saviour brought us to birth.'[1] St Francis seemed to sense wonders in store for the Visitation Order. 'Believe me, my dear Mother,' he wrote to St Jane, 'God means us for something great, you can be sure of that';[2] and to Mother Favre: 'I have an overwhelming confidence in our Lord's grace: in his all-powerful hand this humble, little Institute will be blessed beyond all human calculation.'[3]

Scarcely half a century passed before the appearance of St Margaret Mary, who gave meaning and weight to those words, adding to the presentiments of St Francis the halo of prophecy. St Margaret Mary's name is inseparably linked with devotion

---

[1] *Oeuvres complètes* (Annecy Edition), Vol. XV, letter cdxciii, pp. 63-64. Could it be more than a coincidence that 10 June 1611 was the Friday after the octave of Corpus Christi? This was the day which our Lord later asked should be kept as the feast of the Sacred Heart.
[2] *Oeuvres*, Vol. XVI, letter mxlix, p. 311.
[3] *Oeuvres*, Vol. XVII, letter mclxviii, p. 151.

to the Sacred Heart. Were it not for the work to which God destined her, this obscure French nun would be—as she so dearly wished—utterly unknown.

What was she like, this Saint who was the contemporary of Corneille, Racine, Molière, Bossuet, Bourdaloue and Fênelon in her own country, and of Crashaw, Milton, Bunyan, Dryden and Pope, Herbert and Donne in England; whose life-span enclosed the reign of Louis XIV in France and the events leading up to his inglorious peace with William of Orange, and over here the reign of Charles II and the so-called Titus Oates' plot; who was about to be cured of a childhood sickness by our blessed Lady when St Vincent de Paul died in Paris, and had just experienced four revelations of the Sacred Heart by the time Bl Oliver Plunket was martyred at Tyburn? Fr C. C. Martindale, S.J., in the year of her canonisation, penned a fearlessly penetrating word-picture[1] of this simple little Sister of the Visitation who contrasted so vividly with the proud Angélique Arnaud of Port Royal, the ice-bound Jansenistic atmosphere of which was eventually to melt under the influence of Paray's eucharistic rays:

There is but little charm in Margaret Mary; rarely light-heartedness; merriment rarely; unless I err, never a sense of humour. Dare I suggest, with utter reverence for a Saint whose help I have always asked, that without overwhelming grace, she would have grown up in easy circumstances empty-headed and frivolous; in hard conditions stupid and cowed? In her is no trace of originality nor independence. . . . Nothing is more forced and reforced upon her by direct consciousness, by Superiors' admonitions and by revelation, than her personal futility; her inadequacy even for ordinary life, still more for a public, enduring Church-wide mission. Blank canvas before God, Christ's wax, his toy, his hand-ball; so will she feel herself. We shall not wonder then to find in the expression of her highest visions even—that she is *colloquial* constantly, ungrammatical at times, awkward and ill-arranged in style is a personal matter merely—no turn of phrase, no mannerism, no tiniest sentence unmarked by the purest conventions of the seventeenth century. . . .

[1] In *The Tablet*, 22 May 1920.

The classicism of the French Renaissance was exuberant and showed true temperament; that of the Empire was shoddy imitation; this singular seventeenth century, though points of originality project both in its austerities and in its decoration, was extraordinarily obedient to its own conventions, and of its children none more so than this Saint. She reflects almost textually her authors. The same rhythm, metaphors, false antitheses, conceits even, whether it be she who speaks, or the Saints, or Mary, or our Lord. That she could understand. So by a tender condescension, our Lady to Bernadette spoke *patois*. Is all this supercilious? Please God, far from it. I believe our Lord meant exactly what he said when he repeated to her that by an instrument wholly inappropriate, he meant to renew his Church. I feel that the *abstract Saint* that Margaret Mary too often seems, woos us but weakly; the very simple, very frightened, often unhappy girl bidden to speak Christ's secret to the world and to 'renew his Church', is a figure of enthralling pathos; and her one power of loving, with all it meant of suffering and obedience, vindicates a thousand times the better, when we see the lack of all the rest, our humble veneration.

St Margaret Mary was not the first Saint to experience visions of the Sacred Heart; but she is the latest, and she bears a message for a world grown cold towards God. Her own personality did not matter greatly: she was the insignificant messenger proclaiming the King's message; she was the little secretary taking down the divine dictation; she was the medium whose function it was to pass unnoticed until she had served her purpose. Her mission was a difficult one. She had to persuade the ecclesiastical authorities to institute a special feast in honour of the Sacred Heart; she had to introduce the devotions of the First Fridays and the Holy Hour; and finally, she had to remind the world of its duty of reparation. A tall order, you would say, for an enclosed nun. But this was not all. So that she could claim a hearing, it was necessary for her to be unusual—to have revelations, to experience the higher forms of prayer, to practise excessive mortification. God chose to emphasise this by calling her into a religious Order where the rule was specifically designed to avoid those very things.

St Francis de Sales wished the Visitation nuns to go to God by ordinary ways and by the faithful practice of what he called 'little virtues'; they were never to desire extraordinary favours. It was quite obvious that Margaret Mary was not the ideal Visitation type. She would never have been finally accepted, had it not been equally obvious that she was obedient and humble. Her heroic practice of those two virtues convinced the authorities that nothing human or diabolical was responsible for what was happening to her, and that God was using her to carry out his plans—plans which were to involve the Visitation in something wonderful, and fruitful for the spiritual lives of millions, beyond even the dreams of St Francis.

God never gives anyone a task without also giving the individual everything necessary to accomplish it. He chose St Margaret Mary to reawaken the love of God in human hearts, and he prepared her for this role by purification and by suffering. When she was only four years old, he inspired her to make a vow of chastity; all through her life she was to go on purifying her affections and detaching herself from people and things around her. Failures, of course, she had—for she was human. Tiny resistances to grace, tardiness of response to God's attractions, the little weaknesses of human nature—all these were there; but, deep down in her soul, there was an ever-growing purity and a deeper sharing in the holiness of God. She tells us herself that God drained her will of malice, so that he could possess her heart fresh and pure, before the world could trap it. But she had to pay for this by suffering. She suffered from family difficulties and bereavements; she never enjoyed the best of health; she was considered something of an oddity, both at home and in the convent; she was often misunderstood and thwarted, even when she felt most conscious of following God's will. She was destined to grow more and more like Jesus in his sufferings. He suffered freely and willingly, and love was his motive. So it was with Margaret Mary. God did not force her; he *offered* her the role of victim, and she accepted when she chose the portrait of suffering in preference to the portrait of joy.

The more nearly souls approach the holiness of God, and the more clearly they see themselves in the light of God's truth, the greater becomes their awareness of their littleness, their unworthiness and their lack of response to God's love. Margaret Mary, accustomed to living in the presence of the holiness of God's love and justice, judged herself by those strict standards peculiar to the Saints. She could always hear our Lord saying: 'I am a holy Master, and I teach holiness. I am pure, and I cannot bear the least stain.' That is why, looking back on her childhood, she saw the little indiscretions of those years magnified enormously, despite the fact that after her death her confessors affirmed that she had preserved her baptismal innocence. That is why, too, she could never satisfy her desire for penance, for mortification—a desire which seemed to drive her to unnatural ways of gratifying it. If we find all this so hard to understand, it is simply because sin is not the horror for us that it is for those pure souls whose hearts are broken in the presence of the unloved God.

Our first reaction to St Margaret Mary and the story of her life may well be very definite: here is a Saint to be admired, but certainly not imitated. Undoubtedly, there is much in what she reveals about herself that is beyond our range. Without a special inspiration from God, and the most careful scrutiny on the part of those whom God sends to guide us, we should be very ill-advised to attempt to imitate her penances and even some of her devotional practices. But there is one thing—apart from her virtues—that we can and should imitate: indeed, it is an important part of her message from God. We can all try to acquire the spirit of reparation—a practice underlined by every pope who has written about devotion to the Sacred Heart in recent years.

Reparation involves returning God's love, a love that meets with indifference or coldness from so many souls—even those set apart for God's special service. It also involves spending oneself for the salvation of souls by prayer and penance. The world is full of people who commit sin, and are not sorry for it; who offend God, and never repent; or who have their sins forgiven, and yet never do penance. Christian mortification is not an end in itself; it is only a means to charity, to love. Saints do not crucify their flesh and its concupiscence because crucifixion is an ideal. Rather, they see *through* the cross: they love something beyond the cross, and for that they are willing to suffer pain. Our Lord, in his passion, showed us God loving man; the Saints, in their sufferings and their sacrifices, show us man loving God. Devotion to the Sacred Heart reunites those two which should be one. The Reformation, and all that went with it, separated religion from life—distinguished God from love. So God willed to show anew his personal interest in the lives of those he made because he loved them, and to reveal his longing for them to return his love through personal intimacy with the Word made flesh.

St Margaret Mary was not writing for publication when she composed her autobiography. She would never have put pen to paper without a definite command. Her director, Fr Francis Rolin, S.J.,[1] put her under obedience to write, and in the very first lines she admits her distaste for the task. Father Rolin, who knew that she had burned previous autobiographical details which she had been asked to write, forbade her to burn anything this time until he had examined it. He left Paray a year later, before Margaret had finished writing and before he had seen the MS. It was never completed, for Margaret did not write another word once the priest had gone. On her deathbed she was worried by the fear that others might read it, and begged Sister Péronne Rosalie de Farges to burn it for her. Fortunately, Sister de Farges persuaded the dying Saint—as a final sacrifice of her own will—to give her Superior the key to the cupboard where the MS was kept. The authenticity

---

[1] Resident in Paray, as Superior of the Jesuit house there, 1683-4 and 1685-6. It was during his second term of office that he asked St Margaret Mary to write her autobiography.

of this MS, still preserved at Paray, has twice been affirmed by
ecclesiastical authority—22 July 1715 and 26 February 1865—
when it was severely scrutinised for the process of beatification.
Nothing contrary to orthodox doctrine or Christian living was
discovered, the Church assures us, and the revelations—
together with the devotions springing from them—can be safely
and prudently accepted.[1]

St Margaret Mary's autobiography proves uncomfortable
reading in places, and contains passages that can only apply to
chosen souls. Be that as it may, the following pages allow us
to look wonderingly and humbly into the soul of a Saint. They
give us the first-hand account of the revelations of the Sacred
Heart—and are invaluable for this alone. They also underline
something St Francis de Sales once said from the pulpit, as he
described the happiness which the sight of our Lord will give
us in heaven:

> This, surely, will bring an intensification of bliss which there
> are no words to describe. We cannot imagine what it will
> mean to us, how we shall feel, as we gaze through the wound
> in his pierced side at the vision of our Master's Heart—the
> Heart that calls for love and adoration; the Heart on fire
> with love for us; the Heart in which we shall read our names
> —inscribed, all of them, in letters of love. My name in his
> Heart!—the love of Jesus will leave us wondering; but there
> will be no doubt about it. The prophet was speaking in our
> Lord's name, when he said: ' What, can a woman forget her
> child that is still unweaned, pity no longer the son she bore
> in her womb? Let her forget; I will not be forgetful of thee.
> Why, I have cut thy image on the palm of my hands.' These
> words will grow in the telling as Jesus repeats them to us in
> heaven: ' What, can a woman forget her child? Let her
> forget; I will not be forgetful of thee. Why, I have cut thy
> name deep in my Heart.' There it is, the ultimate consola-
> tion: our Lord loves us so dearly, we have an indelible place
> in his Heart. . . .

---

[1] It should be noted that the Church never guarantees private revelations on her
infallible authority, but only declares that they contain nothing contrary to faith or
morals. There is only one revelation of which the Church is the infallible guardian
—that of our Lord himself.

Let us make our way, then, cheerfully and happily through the difficulties of this fleeting life. Let us welcome with open arms all the mortifications and trials that we shall meet along the road. They will not last, we can be sure of that; death will put an end to them eventually, and we shall go to a new life which knows only joys unfailing, perfect satisfaction and eternal peace.[1]

VINCENT KERNS, M.S.F.S.

[1] Sermon on the second Sunday in Lent, 20 February 1622, *Oeuvres*, Vol. X, sermon lvii, pp. 243-247.

TRANSLATOR'S PREFACE

I T is exactly ten years since I visited Paray-le-Monial for a solemn Triduum in preparation for the feast of St Margaret Mary on 17 October. I can still visualise the Visitation Monastery and the little parlour—the one St Margaret Mary used on her first visit to Paray—in which I spoke to the Mother-superior and the Novice-mistress. I told them of my ambition to attempt a new English version of the *Autobiography* —a suggestion which they received with enthusiasm.

At long last, after two or three abortive attempts, my task is done. It has not proved easy. Margaret's French presents other difficulties besides its age: incorrect grammar, long and involved sentences, incomplete or obscure phrases. Her aim, after all, was not a literary masterpiece; she had very little time for writing, and probably never read over what she had once written. She was writing because she was told to write; and, had it been left to her, the MS would certainly not exist today.

The copybook used for the purpose, and which Margaret kept under lock and key, is now one of Paray's greatest treasures; it is about 7″ × 9″ and contains 64 pages closely written in her own clear hand. In making the present translation, I have used the transcript by Mgr Francis Leo Gauthey, Archbishop of Besançon, which was first published in 1915.[1]

In order to break up the MS into convenient parts and facilitate reference, Mgr Gauthey introduced 111 marginal headings into the text. On reflection, I decided to omit these and divide the text into chapters, as being more in conformity with modern practice.[2] Footnotes are a necessary nuisance, and

[1] *Vie et Oeuvres de Sainte Marguerite Marie Alacoque*, II, pp. 29-119.
[2] The original MS has no divisions.

I have been unable to exclude them. Some people prefer them at the foot of the respective pages; others like them at the back of the book. I have compromised here. Shorter factual notes will be found on the page concerned—indicated by a numeral in the text; longer textual notes are at the back and indicated in the text by an asterisk.

St Margaret Mary does not record in the story of her life all the promises which our Lord made to those who practise devotion to the Sacred Heart; but she mentions them in her correspondence. For this reason, I have included in the Appendices extracts from four of her letters referring to these rewards. Also, in the Appendices, you will find a short biographical note on Bl Claude de la Colombière, and a chronological table for those who wish to know exactly when things happened—St Margaret Mary is often rather vague about the sequence of events.

It only remains for me to express my deep gratitude to the Reverend Joseph Davis, M.S.F.S., S.T.L., and the Reverend Hugh Montgomery, M.A., for their patient and helpful criticisms; and to Mr L. J. Sullivan, editor of the *Catholic Fireside*, for allowing me to make a trial run of this translation in his pages.

Salesianum, 1959.

J'adore Du profond de mon âme le sacre nom de iesus nom cy venerable aux anges cy terrible aux demon & cy plein de vertu & de consolation pour leglise

ste Marie Marguerite Lacoque

A reproduction of St Margaret Mary's writing. The original is at the Visitation Monastery at Paray-le-Monial.

CHAPTER I

TYRANNICAL HOME-LIFE

I TAKE up my pen out of obedience; it is only because I love you, my God, that I am letting myself set down the story of my life. Please forgive me for doing all I could to escape the task. You are the only one to whom I can turn for encouragement; no one else knows how much I hate writing all this. It is from your hands, as a punishment, that I have accepted the obedience. After all, I've always tried too hard to humour my longing for permanent burial from human memory. I had even got one or two useful people to promise to help, and I'd burned all that I'd been allowed to keep of what I had previously written under obedience. Then, out of the blue, came this latest order. Guide my pen, good Jesus, so that every single line I write may bring you glory and increase my shame.

There is so much I owe you, Jesus, my only Love, isn't there? From babyhood on you headed me off, claiming my heart for your very own—though you knew all along how difficult I was going to be. At the dawn of consciousness you showed me the ugliness of sin. So horrible was the impression it left on me, I simply couldn't bear the slightest stain. To check my boisterousness as a child, all they had to do was tell me I was offending God: that used to pull me up short and tear me away from what I'd been bent on doing. Over and over again I found myself saying something I couldn't understand: 'To God I give my purity, and vow perpetual chastity.' Once I said it at Mass between the two elevations.* (I used to hear Mass on my bare knees, even in the coldest weather.) I'd no

3

idea what I had done—neither 'vow' nor 'chastity' meant anything to me—but I knew what I wanted. . . . I wanted to hide in some wood, and only one thing stopped me: I was afraid of coming across men.

The blessed Virgin always watched over me very carefully. I used to take all my needs to her, and she saved me from many a grave danger. I was too shy of approaching her divine Son, but always went to her. I used to offer her my rosary, as a little crown, saying it on my bare knees or genuflecting and kissing the ground at each Hail Mary.

I was very young when I lost my father. Mother was left to provide for his five children, of whom I was the only girl.[1] This meant that she couldn't spend much time at home; so my only education, until I was about eight-and-a-half, came from servants and villagers.

I was sent to a convent. There, when I was about nine, I was prepared for my first Communion. After that Communion all my little treats and toys seemed such sorry things, I couldn't enjoy them any more—though this didn't stop me looking forward to them eagerly. But it always happened, just as I was going to enjoy myself with my companions, that I would feel something pulling me back, calling me away into some little corner, and giving me no peace until I had obeyed. I'd feel drawn to pray, then, on my knees or genuflecting from time to time, as long as I wasn't seen—I simply couldn't bear anyone to find me at it. I always wanted so much to do everything I saw the nuns doing. They were all saints, I was sure; and I thought that, if I were a religious, I should be the same. This made me so keen to imitate them, I could live only for the day when I might join them. I didn't really feel that they were secluded enough for my purpose;* but, as I didn't know any others, I used to tell myself I'd have to stay there.

I was only left in this convent for two years, because then I fell ill. I was so pitifully weak that for nearly four years I couldn't walk. My bones were sticking out of my skin all over.

[1] Her younger sister, Gilberte, born in 1649, had died in 1655.

As no cure could be found for my illness, it was suggested I dedicate myself to the blessed Virgin—promising that, if she cured me, I would eventually be one of her daughters. As soon as I had made this vow, I was better; and, together with my health, I recovered our Lady's protection. She became the mistress of my heart, taking charge of me as her own property, correcting my faults and teaching me to do God's will. And once, when I was sitting down saying my rosary, she stood there in front of me. Very young though I was, when all this happened, I've never forgotten the reproof she gave me: 'I am surprised, child, that you are so careless in my service!' The impression these words left on me was so great as to have been an inspiration all my life.

My one thought, after I was well again, was to make the most of my delicious freedom; and I didn't pay much attention to keeping my promise. But what I failed to remember then, Lord, you clearly brought home to me since. I came to learn what it cost your sacred Heart to bring me to birth on Calvary; that the only source of nourishment for this new life is the cross; and that suffering was to become my favourite food. I can see it all so plainly now. . . . At the first thrill of physical well-being I fell in love with worldly things, persuading myself that the tenderness mother and my brothers showed me gave me a free hand to fasten on all my little treats and enjoy myself to my heart's content. Then you opened my eyes and showed me what a long way out I was. Naturally fond of pleasure, I'd simply pleased myself. I hadn't done what you wanted, and you had something very different in mind.

It was when mother ceased to have any authority in her own house.* . . . She'd been forced to hand it over to others. With the reins in their hands, we were neither of us little better than prisoners. (However, I don't want it to appear—from what I am going to say—that I blame them; I don't think they were wicked to make me suffer as I did. God never let this idea enter my head; I saw them only as instruments of his will.) Well, we hadn't any further say in the running of the house, and we didn't dare do anything without permission. It was one long fight. Everything was under lock and key; often I couldn't even find anything to wear to Mass, and had to borrow both hat and coat. That was when I began to feel my imprisonment. I was so completely tied, I never did anything, nor went out, unless the three of them agreed to it.[1]

This was the turning-point in my search for pleasure. I began to find my comfort in the Blessed Sacrament. Our village was a long way from the church, however, and I could go only if the people I have just mentioned let me; and it used to turn out that when one was willing, another wasn't. Often, when I used to cry for sheer disappointment, I'd be accused of having arranged to meet some boys. I was upset, I'd be told, because I couldn't go and see them—my anxiety to get to Mass or Benediction was merely a pretence; kisses and caresses were what I was really after. (As though I'd even dream of it! I had such a horror of all that sort of thing, I'd rather have been torn to pieces.) All I could do, at times like these, was run off and hide in a corner of the garden or the cowshed, or some other secluded spot, where I could get down on my knees and tearfully open my heart to God. I used to ask the help of our Lady's prayers—my good Mother, in whom I'd placed all my trust. I'd stay there like that, without food or drink, for days at a time; in fact, it was so common a thing that some of the poor village folk took pity on me, and sometimes in the evening would bring me a little milk or fruit. I used to go back to the house in such fear and trembling, I might have been a poor criminal going up for sentence. I'd have been much happier begging my bread than living like that—for, many a time, I didn't dare take anything at table. The moment I entered the house the battle would start all over

<hr>

[1] These three people, whom Margaret in her perfect spirit of charity is careful not to name, were: 1st, her father's mother, Jeanne Delaroche, widow of Claude Alacoque (Margaret's grandmother); 2nd, her father's sister, Benoîte Alacoque, wife of Toussaint Delaroche (Margaret's aunt); 3rd, her father's aunt, Benoîte de Meulin, widow of Simon Delaroche and mother of Toussaint (Margaret's great-aunt)—she was sometimes called ' Mother Chappendye ' after her birthplace.

again worse than ever: I had neglected the housekeeping, my benefactors would complain, or I hadn't looked after their children. Then, without being given any chance of defending myself, I would be set to work with the servants.

I used to spend the nights, after all that, as I had spent the days—crying in front of my crucifix. There, though I didn't understand it at the time, our Lord explained that his aim was the undisputed mastery of my heart, and that my earthly life would be one of suffering like his. He would become my Master just for this: to make me aware of his presence, so that I'd behave as he did during his own cruel sufferings, which—he showed me—he had endured for love of me. (The effect on my soul was so deep, I wouldn't have had my sufferings cease, even for a moment.) He never left me afterwards, and I'd always see him crucified or carrying his cross. In the pity and love that filled my heart, all my own troubles seemed light. Besides, I wanted them; I wanted to take after Jesus in his sufferings. I couldn't bear to see hands, often raised to strike me, stayed from venting the full force of their displeasure. I couldn't resist doing all sorts of services and good turns to my soul's true friends. I'd willingly have made any sacrifice for them, only too happy to speak kindly of them and do anything I could to help them.

I talk as though I did all this, don't I? But it wasn't so; my royal Master was at work in what I am writing about much against my will. He'd taken control of my will, and he wouldn't let me complain or grumble or show any resentment towards these people. He wouldn't even allow anyone to feel sorry for me or show me any pity; that wasn't the way he'd been treated, he said. He wanted me to make excuses for those who harassed me—when I couldn't stop others criticising them—and take all the blame myself. After all, if the truth be told, my sins deserved far worse.

CHAPTER II

HER MOTHER'S ILLNESS
FIRST LESSONS IN PRAYER

I HAVE to force myself to write all this. I've always tried
to make sure it would never leak out—even trying to forget
it myself, content that God does not forget. When I complained of this distaste to my good Master, he made it quite
plain. 'What you feel,' he told me, 'doesn't matter one way
or the other. Go ahead, carry on; my will must be done.'

'But, Lord,' I said, 'how can I possibly remember what
happened more than twenty-five years ago?'

'Don't you know that I am my heavenly Father's eternal
memory,' he replied. 'I forget nothing, and the past and the
future are like the present to me. So don't be afraid; simply
write to my dictation. I promise you, I'll distil my grace into
your words, so that they bring me glory. I have three reasons
for asking this of you. First of all, to show you that all your
efforts in hiding my graces leave me cold; you are a poor,
puny creature, and yet I have enriched you with graces enough
and to spare; never lose sight of them, and you will always
be grateful to me. Secondly, to teach you that these graces are
not to be treated as your own private property, nor are you
to be niggardly in sharing them with others; my plan is to use
you as a conduit to carry graces I have in mind for souls; I
shall show you later how this will rescue many of them from
the very brink of hell. Thirdly, to let you know that I am the
eternal Truth, with whom there is no deception; I am faithful

to my promises, and the graces I have given you can stand any kind of test and trial.'

These words gave me courage. Though I was still in mortal terror of anyone reading these pages, I made up my mind to go ahead with them, cost what it may, so as to fulfil my royal Master's will. . . . My worst cross was seeing no way of making my mother's crosses lighter—I found hers a hundred times harder to bear than my own. It would have been a relief to let her talk about them; but I didn't dare, in case we offended God by the satisfaction of discussing our troubles. It was when she was ill that I felt it most. She was forced to depend on me for care and attention; my efforts didn't amount to much, and so she suffered a lot. The worst of it was that everything was so often locked up; I had even to go and beg for eggs and other things a sick person would need. Naturally shy, I found this quite an ordeal—especially with the villagers, who often had more to say than I'd want to hear.

Once, mother had a dangerous attack of erysipelas on her face. It was dreadfully severe, all swollen and inflamed, and all they did was have her bled by some passing village surgeon of no great ability. Nothing less than a miracle, he told me, would see her well again. No one seemed in the least upset, and I was the only one who bothered about her. I didn't know where to turn. In need of help, I could think only of my usual refuge—the blessed Virgin and my royal Master. There was no one else with whom I could share my constant anxiety;* derision, insults and accusations were all the help I got from those around me. When I went to Mass on the feast of our Lord's Circumcision, to ask him to be poor mother's doctor and make her well, and also to teach me what I ought to do for her, he couldn't have been more sympathetic.

As soon as I got home, I found that the swelling on her cheek had burst. It left an open wound about the size of the palm of my hand, but the stench of it was so unbearable that no one would go near her. I'd no idea of how to dress a wound —I'd never been able to bring myself to look at or touch one before. My only ointment, in any case, was my trust in divine Providence. All I could do each day was scrape off huge lumps of the bad flesh; but I was full of courage and trust in our Lord's goodness, and he seemed to be always at my side. Only a few days later, though (humanly speaking) there wasn't the ghost of a chance, the wound had healed.

All the time mother was ill, I hardly went to bed or slept at all. I took scarcely any food, often going for whole days without tasting a thing. It was my divine Master who kept me going and brought me comfort, helping me to fit in with his holy will. He was the one to whom I clung through it all, with the words: 'Royal Master, if you hadn't wished it, this wouldn't have happened. Thank you for allowing it, so as to make me more like you.'

Meanwhile, I was being drawn to mental prayer. The urge was so strong, it hurt. I didn't know how to set about this form of prayer; and I couldn't learn, for I'd no opportunity of talking to anyone spiritually-minded. The expression 'mental prayer' was all I had to go on, but it charmed me. I appealed to my royal Master, and he taught me his way—the one I've used all my life. This was to humble myself in his presence, asking pardon for all my sins; then, after an act of adoration, to offer him my prayer—though I'd no very clear idea of where to go from there. He'd let me see him, after that, under whatever aspect he wanted me to think of him. My mind would be so riveted to him, all the powers of my soul absorbed in him, that I used to have no distractions. All I felt was an overwhelming desire to love him; and this gave me a longing for holy Communion and for suffering, which I could never satisfy. But I still didn't know what to do. . . . The only time I had was at night, and I used to spend as much of this as I could in prayer. I can't describe how happy it made me; only it wasn't my idea of mental prayer—and that was the urge that gave me no peace. I promised my good Master that, as soon as he had taught me the art, I'd give all the time to it I could.

Well, he kept me so hard at what I've just been describing that I lost all taste for vocal prayers. I simply couldn't say any before the Blessed Sacrament; I used to be so intent on the Real Presence, I was never bored. Days and nights could have come and gone, food and drink forgotten—I wouldn't have noticed it, content to burn out there like a candle and give back love for love. I couldn't stay at the back of the church; I had to get as near the Blessed Sacrament as possible, in spite of the embarrassment I used to feel. The only people I envied were those who could go often to Communion and be free to stay with the Blessed Sacrament—that was my idea of happiness; though, of course, if the truth be told, my time there was not at all well spent, and I'm afraid I must often have put our Lord to the blush. I tried hard to win the friendship of the people I've already mentioned, so that they'd give me a few free moments for visits to the Blessed Sacrament.

But my sins were punished. . . . I could never sleep on Christmas Eve. At midnight Mass the parish priest used to give out that no one could go to Communion who hadn't been to sleep.[1] This left me out; and I never dared to make my Christmas Communion. For me, this merry day was always one of tears—that was my share of the feasting and games. But then, I really had been very wicked. Once, at carnival time, when I was with some other girls, I assumed a disguise out of a false idea of being good-natured. I've bitterly regretted this all my life. Then there was the other fault I used to commit from the same motive—decking myself out in worldly fashions to oblige the people I've already referred to. God was using these same people as instruments of his justice, demanding reparation for my sins. They were good people and had no bad intention in acting as they did towards mother and me. That it was none of their own doing, I'm sure, for God willed it so; and I bore them no grudge.

---

[1] The strange but popular belief that one must have slept before approaching the altar rails on Christmas night was fairly common at that time, and evidently it was shared by the parish priest of Vesrovres, M. Antoine Alacoque.

CHAPTER III

THE INSISTENT CALL

HAVE pity on my weakness, Lord! You make me feel so sorry and ashamed, as I write, for my continued reluctance this long while past to set down the story of my life. Uphold me, my God, else I shall faint from the severity with which you rightly take me to task. Though death, scorn or all hell's fury be the only means of settling this account, by the help of your grace I won't refuse you again, I assure you. Forgive me for being so difficult in the past; give me strength to finish what you want me to do—my self-love will find it much against the grain.

Well, to go on with my story. . . . As I grew up, my crosses got bigger. The devil, to make me break my vow of chastity, led several eligible young men to think of marrying me. This meant that we often had callers, and I had to see them all. I was on the rack now, and no mistake. Down here was the family, urging me to get married—mother, most of all; she never stopped crying; I was her only hope of happiness, she said, of getting away—once I was settled in a home of my own, she would be able to come and live with me. Up there was God, fighting for my heart and giving no quarter; my vow—I couldn't forget that; there'd be frightful punishments in store for me, if I proved unfaithful. The devil, taking advantage of my fondness for mother, kept me concentrating on her tears. . . . If I became a nun, she'd die of grief; and I'd be responsible. Mother had no one else to look after her, and I'd have to answer to God for what I did. . . . I couldn't bear it; we loved each other so much, we were inseparable. But I was still haunted by the idea of becoming a nun, and by my horror of impurity. I went through martyrdom.

Unable to make up my mind, I had no one to confide in, no rest from this ordeal, and I used often to burst into tears. In the end, my tender feelings towards mother, dear good soul, began to gain the upper hand. After all, I thought to myself, when I made that vow I was only a child; I didn't really understand what I was doing; surely, I could easily get a dispensation! Besides, I dreaded having to give up my freedom. I'd try to persuade myself that becoming a nun would mean the end of all my fastings, almsgivings and scourgings, just when I liked; the religious life would demand a great personal holiness I could never reach—by going into a convent, I'd only lose my soul. So I began to go about more, dressing attractively, and doing my best to have a good time.

You, my God, were the only witness to the extent and duration of that frightful struggle going on inside me. I'd have given in a thousand times over without the special help you were good enough to give, taking pity on me. Your plans for me were very different from mine. You made it quite clear to me then, as at other times, that I could only hurt myself by kicking against the powerful goad of your love. But, spiteful and unfaithful as I was, I strained every effort to resist and stifle its slightest impulse. It was no use, however. . . . I'd be enjoying myself with my friends—when, suddenly, like so many burning arrows, your love would pierce my heart and set it all on fire. This used to leave me speechless with pain.

Still, it took more than that to get as thankless a heart as mine to leave off struggling. I had to be roped and dragged, it would seem, until I'd no choice but to follow him. He was calling me to some place of privacy, where he could take me severely to task. It was my wretched, tortured heart he wanted —and wanted for his own. Flat on my face, I had to ask his pardon; and then he'd make me take a severe and lengthy discipline. Straight back to my frivolities I'd go, after that, and continue being difficult exactly as before. At night, when I took off the devil's uniform—my tawdry finery which pandered to his evil purpose—I'd see my royal Master there before me, mutilated from his scourging. The bitterness of his reproofs! . . . This was what my frivolity had done to him; I was wasting precious time for which I'd have to give a strict account when I came to die; I was a traitor, hounding him to death, and all that he had done was prove how much he loved me and wanted me to grow to be like him! . . . These words used to bite home until my heart ached so much that I would break down and cry. I don't think I could put into words very easily all that I had to go through.

I had no idea of the spiritual life. It had never figured in my lessons, and I'd never even heard it mentioned. All I knew was what my divine Master taught me, his love forcing me on. I wanted, somehow, to teach myself a lesson. I had hurt my Master; and I wanted to get back to being more like him. As much to ease my inner pain as anything, I tied knotted cords round my guilty body, pulling them so tight, I could hardly eat or breathe. The flesh grew over them, I left them like that for such a long time, and only brute force could remove them —an agonising process. The same thing happened to the tiny little chains which I fastened round my arms; they cut into my flesh when I tried to get them off. In addition, I used to sleep on a board, or else I'd make a bed out of sticks full of sharp knots. Then there was the discipline; I used to take that, too. I had to find some relief from my inner conflict and its agony. The pain that came from outside—and I was now being even more humiliated and thwarted in the ways I've already described—this pain seemed a refreshing change after all that I was going through inside. Trying to prove an apt pupil for my good Master, I forced myself to endure it all in silence and keep it a secret. Looking at me, you wouldn't have noticed anything—except that I seemed to grow paler and thinner.

What distressed me most of all, though, was my fear of offending God. There seemed to be no end to my sins—and such big ones! I was amazed that hell didn't open at my feet to swallow me up, I felt so wicked. I'd have liked to go to confession every day, but I could only manage it now and then. They were saints, I thought, the people who spent a long time in the confessional; and not at all like me. I didn't know how to accuse myself of my sins; and it upset me very much. The inner conflict, and my various other sufferings, went on for several years. I had only one source of comfort all that time—our Lord Jesus Christ, who had become my Master and guide. Then, suddenly, the desire to be a nun flared up once more. So strong was it this time, I definitely made up my mind to enter, cost what it might. Unfortunately, another four or five years were to pass before this could be realised.[1] Meanwhile, all my sufferings and difficulties became twice as bad; but I did my best, as far as our Lord would let me, to redouble my penances.

As a matter of fact, our Lord brought about a great change in me. He gave me a deeper appreciation of the beauty of virtue—especially poverty, chastity and obedience, the three vows of religion. It is the keeping of these vows, he told me, that makes saints . . . you see, when I said my prayers I used to ask him to make me a saint. My usual reading was a book of saints' lives; and, every time I opened it, I'd have but one idea—to look for someone it would be very easy to copy. I could then do everything she did, and become a saint too. What used to upset me, though, was the memory of how greatly I had offended God. I was sure this wasn't the case with the saints—or, at least, if an odd one had been a sinner, a lifetime of repentance had followed. If only I could do the same! My divine Master, however, had imbued me with such a fear of following my own will that I was convinced he would be pleased with my efforts in that line only if they were prompted by loving obedience. To love and to obey—that was all I wanted; but I'd no idea how to achieve it. It would be

[1] Since Margaret entered the convent in June 1671, the period she is referring to must be 1666-7, when she was nineteen or twenty—or even a few years earlier.

wrong to tell God I loved him, I used to think, when my actions seemed to belie my words.

I begged our Lord to teach me how he'd like me to please him and show my love for him, and then help me to do it. His answer was to make me very fond of the poor. I'd no desire to mix with anyone else, I came to love them so much. If it had been left to me, I'd have beggared myself for them, God gave me such pity and sympathy for their distress. Whenever I had any money, I'd give it to their little ones. They would flock round me then, these children, and I'd teach them their catechism and their prayers. Sometimes I'd have so many, that in winter I didn't know where to put them. There was only one big room I could think of, and several times we were turned out of there—no small mortification for me, as I wanted to keep what I was doing a secret. People began to think I was giving away to the poor everything I could lay my hands on. (As though I'd have dared!—I was too afraid of stealing for that.) I never parted with anything, unless it belonged to me; and even that, I now felt, needed the sanction of obedience. I was forced to make a fuss of mother to get her to let me give away what I had. Normally, she wouldn't be too difficult about it—she was so fond of me—but if she refused, I'd hold my peace, wait a little, and then return to the attack. I could only bring myself to do anything now, if I had permission. It wasn't just mother I asked; I also put myself under the other people in the house—a constant thorn in my side. It had struck me that I ought to test my vocation by being submissive to those I liked least, obeying them. I picked up a lot of refusals and restrictions, seeking those permissions, and the people involved had me completely under their thumbs; no religious could have been more dependent.

I was so bent on loving God that I managed to get round all these obstacles, and even go out of my way to do the most uncongenial things, the things I'd have been glad to avoid. A definite obligation—that's what I felt I was faced with; and if at any time I failed to follow inspirations of this kind, I used to mention it in confession. I simply couldn't bear the sight of wounds: to cure myself of this, I started to kiss the wounds of the poor and then to dress them. Since I was quite inexperienced, my divine Master had to make up for my ignorance. Even the most alarming wounds healed in a surprisingly short time—God's providence my only ointment; but then, I'd much more confidence in his goodness than in any medicine. I still went out of my way to find what I was naturally fond of—pleasure, amusement; but I couldn't enjoy it any longer. I would see a pitiful figure—my Saviour, fresh from his scourging: it wasn't easy to go on having a good time after that! Especially as I'd hear him saying: 'Are you really so bent on enjoying yourself? I didn't have a good time on earth. Sorrow—sorrow in all its forms—was the lot I chose, trying to win your heart, because I love you. But no, you'll go on fighting me for it.' Quite candidly, though impressed, I was also bewildered by it all; I wasn't very bright, intellectually or spiritually. If any good came from what I did, I've nothing to be proud of; I couldn't help it—my divine Master was the compelling spring of all those deeds of mine.

What I am setting down here fills me with shame. Can't you see that all I deserve is unmitigated eternal punishment? I've tried to hold out against God and put up a long line of barriers to grace. But can't you see the depth of his mercy, too? He had devoted himself to shadowing me—wouldn't you think?—and, at every turn, to meeting spite with kindness, ingratitude with love. The deepest regret of my life—there you have it . . . he came to set me free; he has wrapped me round with his loving care, all the way from my cradle . . . and I couldn't see it.

CHAPTER IV

FAMILY OPPOSITION

ONE day, when our Lord really had me guessing, when I just couldn't understand why all my defects, my lack of loyalty, never seemed to put him off, he'd this answer for me: 'An alloy of my love and mercy—that is what I am going to make you.' 'I chose you for my bride,' he reminded me another time; 'we plighted our troth when you made your vow of chastity. That was my doing—I wanted your heart fresh and pure, before the world could trap it. I even drained your will of malice, so that it could stay like that for me. Then I left you in my Mother's care, for her to fashion to my purpose.'

And a good Mother she has always been to me: no appeal of mine for help ever meets with a refusal. I've always gone to her with my problems and my wants: I could trust her; I felt I had nothing to fear in such a Mother's care. It was at this time that I made her a solemn promise: I'd fast every Saturday; I'd say the Little Office of the Immaculate Conception as soon as I could read it; I'd genuflect seven times a day for the rest of my life, and say seven Hail Marys, in honour of her Seven Sorrows; I'd be her slave, if only she would let me. There was nothing formal about all this—I was simply a little child talking to a good mother, a Mother I've loved truly ever since. When she saw I was once more on the point of giving way to my dreadful inner conflict our Lady took me severely to task.

The family theme-song—girls should make a match at

18

twenty—and dearest mother's tears were proving too much for me, and I was beginning to weaken. Satan, too, never left me alone. ' Poor wretch,' he was always saying, ' what do you want to become a nun for? You'll be the laughing-stock of everyone: you'll never stick it. Fancy having to take off the habit and leave the convent! You wouldn't know where to hide yourself for shame.' It wasn't that I wanted to get married—the very idea of having anything to do with men made me shudder. I used to get so mixed up, I'd burst into tears. But, in the end, my divine Master, who never let me lose sight of my vow, took pity on me. It was one day after Communion, if I remember rightly. . . . He let me see that I'd never find a lover like him—the richest, most attractive and powerful, most perfect and accomplished of all lovers. I'd been promised to him, hadn't I? Why, then, after all these years, did I suddenly want to break it off with him for someone else. ' I give you my word,' he went on; ' scorn me, and I shall have nothing more to do with you . . . ever. Be faithful, and I will never leave you; and I'll make short work of all who oppose you. I am overlooking your ignorance this time; after all, you don't really know me yet. Be true, and follow me, and I shall teach you who I am: I'll show myself to you.'

As he spoke, I felt the disturbance in my heart grow calm— peace of soul at last! I would die, I decided, sooner than change my mind. It was as though my chains had snapped. I had nothing to fear now. If the religious life turned out to be a kind of purgatory* . . . better a lifetime of that than one day to find myself in hell—and that's what my sins and my rebellions have so often asked for. My mind was made up: I was going to be a nun! My divine Bridegroom, however, was afraid I might still give him the slip; would I make over my freedom to him, he wanted to know, and let him take charge of it, seeing my weakness? I was only too happy to agree, and ever since, so firm his grip, I've no longer taken advantage of it. He was so close to me, so much a part of my heart, that I made my vow of chastity all over again—now I was beginning to understand what it was about. Were it to cost me my life a thousand times over, I told him, I'd be a nun—or nothing!

I made no secret of my intentions now. The family were still trying to impress me with the eligibility of one suitor or another, but I would get them to send him away. Even mother dried her eyes—at least, she didn't let me see her tears; but she still shed them whenever anyone spoke to her of my vocation. They never failed to come and tell me then that it would kill her if I went away. . . . I'd have to answer for it to God, since she'd no one else to look after her. . . . Couldn't the convent wait? . . . There was no need to enter while mother was alive. . . . One of my brothers,[1] who was very fond of me and tried all ways to get me to change my mind, even offered some of his own property to make me a better settlement. But all these appeals found my heart hard as a rock—though I had another three years of struggle to face before I could leave the world.

I was sent to live with one of my uncles,[2] who had a daughter[3] a nun. Aware of my plans, she left no stone unturned to get me into her convent; but the Ursuline life held no attraction for me. 'Look,' I told her, 'if I entered your convent, I'd only be doing it for love of you. I want to go where I shall have no family ties, no links with old friends, so that my becoming a nun will be entirely for love of God.' I was very fond of my cousin, and I felt her urgent entreaties would soon wear me down, especially as I'd no idea which Order to join, nor which convent to go to. She persuaded her father to use his influence with me. Since he was my guardian, this uncle of mine, I couldn't bring myself to go against his wishes. He used to tell me he loved me like his own child, and so wanted to have me within reach. Never would he allow my brother to take me home; he was determined, he said, to win me over.

This made my brother very annoyed with me. He hadn't yet

---

1 Chrysostom Alacoque. Margaret's two elder brothers died in infancy; Chrysostom, the third one, took charge of the household when he came of age. The youngest of the family, Jacques, became a priest.
2 Philibert Lamyn, Mme Alacoque's brother.
3 Sister Sainte-Colombe, an Ursuline nun at Mâcon.

agreed to my going into a convent, and he thought I was behind all that intrigue . . . trying to get into the Ursulines in spite of him, and without the family's consent. This was farthest from my thoughts: in fact, the harder they tried to get me to enter there, the less I relished the idea; and a mysterious inner voice kept whispering: ' Not there, not there! I want you at the Holy Marys.'[1] But, in spite of the fact that we had relatives in the Order, I was never allowed to go anywhere near a Visitation convent. I was told things about them guaranteed to daunt the most resolute character; yet the more they tried to put me off, the more I liked the idea. The lovely name—Holy Marys—attracted me, and I felt myself increasingly drawn in that direction. There, I was convinced, I should find what I was looking for. And one day, in front of a picture of the great St Francis de Sales, I felt he was gazing at me lovingly in such a fatherly way, and calling me his child, that I've always thought of him as my good father ever since. I didn't dare breathe a word of this to anyone, and I was at a loss to know how to get away from my cousin and her community. Their kindness was making it impossible for me to resist them any longer.

The convent door was almost standing open for me, when I got a message to say my brother was very ill and mother was dying. There was nothing for it but to leave at once; and they couldn't very well stop me. I had twenty-five miles to go, but I travelled all night. I wasn't well myself at the time—due to fretting, as much as anything; I felt I was being forced into a convent where God wasn't calling me. And so I escaped—but only to shoulder another heavy cross! I won't go into details . . . I've said enough already. I'll just mention that I had to meet twice as many difficulties as before, and leave it at that.

They made it quite clear at home that mother couldn't live without me. I had only to look, they said, at the state to which my brief absence had brought her; I would have to answer for it to God, if she died. This hurt me very much, especially as

[1] This was the name often given to the Visitation nuns in the seventeenth century.

I heard it even from the clergy. I loved mother dearly, and the devil was playing on this to make me believe that, if I went on in this way, I'd lose my soul. Neither was my divine Master giving me any peace. He kept urging me to leave everything and follow him. He made me so keen to imitate him in his sufferings, what I was going through seemed nothing at all; so I set about redoubling my penances. At times, kneeling before my crucifix, I'd tell him: 'It would make me so happy, my dear Saviour, if only you would let me mirror your sufferings.' And he used to answer: 'That is what I mean to do, if you play your part and don't offer any opposition.' I used to bind my fingers tightly and prick them with needles, so that I'd have some blood to give him. Every day I could during Lent I took the discipline in memory of his scourging: as I used to take it on my shoulders, I was a long time drawing blood—and even then there was so very little of it to offer my good Master in return for the blood he shed for love of me. On the three days of carnival[1] I'd willingly have torn myself to pieces to make amends for the crimes sinners were committing against God. I did my best to make bread and water my frugal diet, and gave to the poor the food prepared for me.

[1] In other words, the three days preceding Lent. Cf. note p. 91.

CHAPTER V

PARAY AT LAST

W HAT I looked forward to most, about going into a convent, was being able to go often to Communion. At home, they would only let me go on rare occasions. Frequent Communion!—that was the height of happiness for me. If only they'd have let me spend whole nights alone with the Blessed Sacrament! Though I was a very timid girl, I felt quite safe there; my mind was so full of the happiness it gave me, I couldn't think of anything else. On the eve of each Communion I found it an effort to speak to anyone: the sublimity of what I was going to do plunged me into silent awe. Later, when I had made my Communion, the feeling of peace and happiness was so overpowering that I'd no desire to eat or drink, look at anything, or speak to anyone. I found myself hiding away somewhere, so that I could learn how to love my royal Master, who was compelling me to return his love for me. I felt I'd never manage this, however hard I tried, unless I learned the art of mental prayer—all I knew about that was what our Lord had taught me: to give myself up to the workings of his grace whenever I could be alone with him. But there was never any time: all day long they had me working with the servants; and the evenings would find the household dissatisfied with everything I'd done. I used to get such severe scoldings, I couldn't face any food; and I'd take myself off, at the first opportunity, desperate for a few minutes' peace.

I was dreadfully afraid of failing to please our Lord in

23

everything I did. There was too much of self in it all; even my mortifications were of my own choosing. I couldn't set any store by what I did, you see, unless it were dictated by obedience. 'Lord,' I used to sigh, 'give me a guide—someone to bring me safely home to you.'

'Aren't you satisfied with me?' was his reply. 'What are you afraid of? Your Father in heaven is all-powerful; no child in his arms can ever be lost—especially one I love as much as you.'

Spiritual direction had no meaning for me, but I was anxious to have my life regulated by obedience. Providence took a hand in this, during the Holy Year,[1] when a Franciscan priest stayed the night at our house so that we could make our general confessions. It took me more than a fortnight to write mine: not that it was a new experience for me—I never missed any opportunity of making a general confession—but I always felt I hadn't adequately expressed my sinfulness. I was so deeply sorry for my sins, they not only brought tears to my eyes, but I'd have been glad for them to become public knowledge. What really upset me was my spiritual blindness: I couldn't see my sins properly, nor could I explain how serious they were. That's why I used to write down all the sins I could find in books on confession. Sometimes I even put down sins which I felt were too disgusting to mention. I persuaded myself that I might have committed them unknowingly, or perhaps I'd forgotten about them, and that in any case God's justice demanded the satisfaction of my shame in confessing them. Of course, I didn't really believe I'd committed most of these sins; otherwise I'd have been in despair. That sort of confession would have led there anyway, if my royal Master hadn't assured me that, where there is no malice, all is forgiven. The good father, when the time came, wouldn't let me read it all, this confession of mine. I was a greater sinner than

[1] She is referring to the Jubilee proclaimed by Clement X on the occasion of his election as Supreme Pontiff in 1670. It was granted to the diocese of Autun in 1671, beginning on 22 February—four months before Margaret entered the Visitation convent at Paray.

he thought, I told him, and begged him to let me satisfy my conscience: but no, he made me leave out quite a few pages. As a result of this confession, I found great peace.

I told the priest a little about my way of life—not everything, for I didn't want to appear conceited. I was very much afraid of becoming proud—with my temperament, that was always the danger. I would wonder sometimes if pride wasn't at the root of everything I did; I didn't know then that there is a difference between feeling something and giving way to the feeling. It used to worry me quite a lot; I dreaded the idea of being parted from God by sin. However, the good father made several helpful suggestions, and also promised to let me have some instruments of penance. I went on to tell him about my desire to be a nun; and how, for four or five years, my brother had been preventing me from going into a convent. Whatever the priest said to my brother afterwards, it certainly gave the poor lad scruples. He was soon asking me if that was what I still wanted to do. When I told him I'd sooner die than change my mind, he promised to fix things up for me.

My cousin was still after me to become an Ursuline, so my brother went along there to discuss the business of my dowry. (That was the convent mother and the rest of the family wanted me to enter; and now I could no longer see any way out.) I appealed for help to my mistress, the blessed Virgin, through the intercession of St Hyacinth,* all the time my brother was away; and I had many Masses said in her honour. Then, lovingly, she spoke these words of comfort: 'Have no fear; you will be one of my own daughters, and I shall always be a good mother to you.' So soothing were those words, I hadn't the slightest doubt that it would come true in spite of all the obstacles.

'They want £600,' my brother told me, when he got back. 'Now, it's up to you. I didn't clinch the matter.'*

'Neither shall I!' was my inflexible reply. 'It's the Holy Marys I want to join; and the convent must be a long way off, where I don't know anybody and have no one belonging to me. I want to be a nun entirely for love of God. I want to leave the world completely—to hide myself in some little nook, where I can forget and be forgotten, and never see it again.'

Several monasteries were suggested, but I couldn't make up my mind about any of them. As soon as Paray was mentioned, however, a thrill of joy passed through me; and I agreed at once. But another hard struggle was ahead of me: I still had to see the nuns in the convent where I'd been a boarder when I was eight years old. They took me inside. . . . I was their child, they said, so why did I want to leave them—they were so fond of me! They couldn't stand by and watch me enter the Holy Marys, they added, for they were quite sure I wouldn't stay there long. I was going to try anyway, I told them; but they made me promise to go back to them when I came out. There was no question about it, they repeated, I wouldn't settle down where I was going. . . . Their words were lost on me. I grew only more determined than ever to see it through—and kept on telling myself: ' Succeed, or perish in the attempt! '

I'll spare you all my other struggles—to come straight to dear Paray, where my happiness lay. . . . No sooner had I stepped into the parlour than a voice inside me whispered: ' This is where I want you! ' [1] Turning to my brother, I told him he would have to fall in with my wishes, as there could be nowhere else for me. It was quite a shock for the poor fellow. He had taken me there on the understanding that I was simply going to call on the nuns, and I'd promised not to say anything about wanting to join them. Now, I wouldn't go home until everything was settled!

I was a different person after that. All the happiness and peace I felt made me so gay that I used to overhear people who didn't know my secret exclaim: ' Look at her! Hardly one's idea of a *nun*! ' And, sure enough, I had taken to wearing more pretty things than usual, and I was having a

---

[1] This, Margaret's first visit to the parlour at Paray, seems to have taken place on 25 May 1671.

PARAY AT LAST   27

lot more fun—I was so happy to know that I was completely
God's at last. Again and again, as I write these pages, he
chides me lovingly: ' Where could you find a father, my dear—
so fond of his only child, giving it every care and attention
and proving his love in so many delicate ways—who could
compare with me? I have given you so much, and mean to
give you still more. From babyhood upwards I have been
patiently fashioning you to my liking, undismayed when you
proved difficult, quietly waiting for you to come round. And
remember this: if you ever forget that you owe it all to me,
and that I am the only one to thank for it—though the source
of all good things is inexhaustible, it will dry up for you! '

CHAPTER VI

DAYS OF FEARFUL STRUGGLE

ALL in good time the day came—the day I had been looking forward to so much, the day for bidding the world good-bye. I'd never felt happier, nor more determined; and I was almost indifferent to all the love and tears around me. Mother was more moved than anyone else, but I was quite dry-eyed when the time came to leave. A slave-girl, free now and her chains struck off, taking her place in her Bridegroom's house—that's how I felt. I was beside myself with joy, for our Lord told me to make free of his presence, his blessings and his love. The only reason I could give for my vocation to the Holy Marys was that I wanted to be our Lady's daughter; but I must admit that when the day dawned—it was a Saturday—all my earlier sufferings came back, and more besides. So fierce was this attack that it felt, as I crossed the convent threshold, as if body and soul were being torn apart. Then, all at once, it became clear that our Lord had undone the sackcloth I wore, and was girding me with gladness.[1] In a transport of joy, I exclaimed: 'This is where God wants me!'

Right from the start, I was convinced that this was God's house, a holy place, and that everyone living here ought to be a saint. Holy Mary—the very name made that clear, cost what it might; and it would mean handing oneself over as a perfect victim, keeping nothing back, and spending oneself to the uttermost.

[1] *Conscidisti saccum meum et circumdedisti me laetitia*, Ps. 29:12.

During those first days, the things I found hardest were eased for me by words which woke me up for several mornings: '*Dilexisti justitiam . . .*' and the rest of the verse.[1] Or sometimes: '*Audi filia et vide,* etc.'[2] Or this one: 'Thou hast committed thy life to the Lord wherever thou goest, Jerusalem, race of Israel! The Lord leads thee now; he will not play thee false and forsake thee.'[3] I didn't understand these words, but I heard them distinctly; and I repeated them all, mystifying though I found them, to my Novice-mistress,[4] for I was at pains to view her—and my Superior[5] no less—as it were Jesus in the flesh.* I'd never known what it was to be guided and given spiritual direction, so I was very glad to find myself under obedience. I felt that anything they told me came straight from God, and that obedience to them would free me from any further worry.

I still felt the pangs of spiritual hunger, in my longing to master mental prayer, and so I asked my Novice-mistress to teach me. She just wouldn't believe that I was so ignorant; after all, I was twenty-three when I entered religion. I convinced her it was a fact, and she gave me my first lesson: 'Go; stand before our Lord like a canvas ready for the artist.' I should have liked her to explain what she meant, but I didn't dare tell her I hadn't understood. However, some inner voice called me: 'Come! I will teach you.' No sooner had I settled myself for prayer than my royal Master explained that this canvas was my soul, and that he wanted to paint there a reproduction of his sufferings. His whole life had been one of suffering—a round of love, poverty and loneliness, ending in silence and sacrifice. He would imprint this on me, he said, when he had purified my soul from its remaining stains—attachment

---

1 Ps. 44:8—'Thou hast been a friend to right, an enemy to wrong, and God, thy own God, has given thee an unction to bring thee pride beyond any of thy fellows.'
2 Ps. 44:11—'Listen, my daughter, and consider my words attentively; thou art to forget, henceforward, thy own nation, and the house of thy father; thy beauty, now, is all for the king's delight; he is thy Lord, and worship belongs to him.'
3 Although they echo the Scriptures, these words are not in the Bible.
4 Mother Anne Frances Thouvant. She was a native of Paray-le-Monial; she was also Superior at the convent there for twelve years.
5 Mother Margaret Jerome Hersant. She was Superior at Paray from 1666 to 1672.

to earthly things and that love of self and of creatures for which my good-natured temperament gave me no small inclination. There and then he tore them all away: he emptied my heart and denuded my soul, and then set light to a consuming urge for love and suffering. He gave me no peace, ever haunting me with his love, I couldn't think of anything else but of crucifying myself for love of him; and God has always been so good to me that he has never failed to provide me with the means.

Although I never kept anything back from my Novice-mistress, I thought I might put a wider interpretation on her permission for penances than she intended. I was just setting about doing this, when our holy Founder[1] called a halt. He took me so severely to task, I've never dared to do it again; and his words have always remained deeply imprinted on my heart: ' Really, child! Do you think God will like it, if you overstep the limits of obedience? And obedience, not austerity, is the foundation and mainstay of this Congregation.'

My postulancy was one long desire to receive the habit and belong completely to God; and his loving-kindness saw to it that I was fit for this grace. As I put on the habit, my divine Master made it quite clear that this was our betrothal ceremony. It gave him a further claim on me, and I was now doubly committed to love him above all things. Then, as any passionate lover would, he let me see that during our engagement I should experience only the most loving of his sweet caresses; these, sure enough, were so extravagant, they used to carry me right out of myself until I was unable to move. I was covered with such confusion, I didn't dare show myself; and I was taken to task for it. . . . This wasn't the spirit of the daughters of Holy Mary at all, I was made to understand. Not for them the unusual ways; and unless I dropped all that sort of thing, I couldn't be accepted. This nearly broke my heart. I did everything I could—nothing was too much—to turn aside from that path; but it was all wasted effort.

[1] St Francis de Sales (1567-1622).

My Novice-mistress helped, though I couldn't see it at the time. She understood my craving for mental prayer; and she was not blind to the fact that, try as I would, I couldn't follow the method she was teaching me—I was always going back to my divine Master's way, no matter what I did to forget everything he had taught me. So she appointed me to help a sister entrusted with special duties, who had me working during prayer-time. When I asked the Novice-mistress afterwards if I could make up for this privately, she gave me a severe correction. . . . I was to make my meditation, she said, doing the work of the novitiate. Even so, all the external activity couldn't disturb my spiritual joy and consolation; rather, it seemed to increase it. I was told to leave the choir, after listening to the points of the morning meditation, and get on with the sweeping allotted to me until the hour for Prime. Afterwards, I had to give an account of my prayer—though you couldn't really call it mine, as my royal Master was doing the praying for me; the only thing I could do was obey. All this made me very happy, despite the physical suffering it used to cause, and presently I'd be singing:

> ' Decry my love; Whate'er you say
>   My love will brighter burn:
> Give me no peace by night or day;
>   From him I'll never turn.
> Let sorrow come; 'tis not to part
> But bind me closer to his heart.'

There was no satisfying my hunger for humiliations and mortifications, despite the fact that—with my sensitive nature —I felt them keenly. My divine Master was for ever urging me to ask for them, and this brought me some good ones: although those I asked for were denied me, as I didn't deserve them, they gave me others which I wasn't expecting at all. Indeed, these were so much against the grain—and I, hard put to it to constrain myself—that I was forced to cry out: ' Alas,

D

good Master, come to my aid; after all, it's all your doing! ' As he did so, he warned me: ' Admit that, separated from me, you have no power to do anything. I will never leave you helpless as long as you always keep your nothingness and weakness buried in my strength.'

Only one of these mortifications—one which proved too much for me—is worth mentioning. On that occasion I found our Lord really was as good as his word. . . . There's one thing for which everyone in our family had a natural horror;[1] so much so, it was the only reservation my brother made in the contract drawn up when I entered—they were never to make me do that one thing. (No objection was raised to this, as the matter was of very little consequence.) Yet, that was the very thing I had to face. . . . Everyone created such a fuss about it, I didn't know what to do. Death, I felt, couldn't be half so terrible; and, if my vocation hadn't been dearer to me than life itself, I'd have given up sooner than agree to what they wanted. But it was no use being difficult . . . my royal Master had set his heart on the sacrifice; it was a kind of test case. There were three days of such fearful struggle that everybody felt sorry for me, especially my Novice-mistress. She stood there, while I began trying to do what I was told; but my courage failed me. I was so disappointed at being unable to overcome myself, I could have died. ' Alas,' I told her, ' take my life rather than let me fail in obedience! ' Her answer was to send me from the room. ' Be off with you! ' she said. ' You don't deserve to be obedient; I forbid you now to do what I asked.'

That was all I needed! . . . I blurted out the words, ' Succeed, or perish in the attempt! ' and made for my usual refuge—the Blessed Sacrament. I spent three or four hours there, in tears and sighs, to gain the strength to conquer myself. ' Oh dear, have you forsaken me, my God? Why must I hold something back from my sacrifice! Why can't I provide a perfect holocaust? ' But our Lord was bent on stretching my

---

1 They had an unconquerable loathing for eating cheese.

love to its limits; it was a test of my loyalty, he explained later on. It delighted him to see divine love opposing natural loathing in his unworthy slave. Eventually, however, the field was God's. 'Love can have no limits!'—these words being all I had to arm or encourage myself with, I went back to the Novice-mistress. Down on my knees, I begged her to take pity on me and let me do now what she had asked. In the end, I did it; but I've never known anything so distasteful in all my life. It was the same story all over again each time I had to do this during the next eight years or so.

This first sacrifice of mine resulted in my royal Master redoubling his graces and favours. There was such a flood of them, I was often obliged to exclaim: 'My God, either stay this torrent which is swallowing me up, or enlarge my capacity for it!' But I won't mention all the many ways in which his love allured me; they were so wonderful, I really couldn't describe them.

CHAPTER VII

PROFESSION

IT was drawing near the time for my profession, and all the extraordinary graces I was receiving resulted in a fresh outburst of criticism. I was warned that I was obviously unsuited to the Visitation spirit; such unusual ways were suspect there, as liable to lead to deception and illusion. I lost no time in pointing this out to my royal Master. 'Oh dear, Lord,' I complained, 'are you going to be the cause of my being sent away?'

'Tell your Superior,'[1] he replied, 'that she need have no fears in admitting you to profession. I will answer for you, if she will accept me as surety.'

When I reported this, she ordered me to ask our Lord—as a proof of his surety—to make me an asset to the Order through an exact observance of all its rules. In his loving-kindness, he gave me this answer: 'Of course, you shall have that privilege, my child! Indeed, I am going to make you an even greater asset to the Order than she imagines; but the way in which this will happen is still my secret. In future, I shall adapt my graces to the spirit of your rule, the will of your superiors, and your own weakness. I want you to put the rule before everything else; so be very suspicious of anything that would prevent you from keeping it exactly. Moreover, when your superiors forbid you to carry out my commands, I expect you to put their wishes before mine. Let them do just

---

1 Mother Mary Frances de Saumaise, who belonged to the Visitation Monastery at Dijon. She had just come to Paray as Superior—the first time she held that office—shortly before Ascension Day 1672.

34

what they like with you; I can easily find ways—often seem-ingly the most unorthodox and least likely—of making my plans come true. But the guidance of your spiritual life—*that* I am reserving to myself. Your heart is mine; my love reigns there, and I shall never yield that throne to others.'

This satisfied both my Mother-Superior and the Novice-mistress. In any case, they couldn't very well doubt any longer; it was obvious from the effects of those words that the eternal Truth had spoken. I knew complete peace of soul now; and I simply strove to be obedient, however painful it might prove to be. What I couldn't bear, however, was to have respect and kindness shown to me; that was like a martyrdom. And the way I saw it, such treatment was due punishment for my sins. . . . I was so haunted by the enormity of them that all the tortures you could think of would have been a delicious relief—atoning for my wickedness and appeasing God's justice.

At last the eagerly-awaited blessing of my profession day arrived—the day on which my divine Master really took me as his bride. I can't tell you exactly what happened; all I can say is that I was transfigured, and he seemed to clothe me with an inner radiance. As for my own feelings, I think I should have found death less of a torture, so little did I seem to resemble the vision of my Bridegroom bruised and broken on the cross. Yet this was what he told me: ' There is a time for everything, but leave the care of that to me. Just now, I mean you to be my plaything, for me to do what I like with —as a child would with its toy. So give yourself blindly and unreservedly to me—there, at my disposal, whenever I feel like it. You won't lose by it.' Promising never to leave me, he added: ' Always keep yourself ready, waiting for me; in future, I am going to make my home in your heart, where we can talk and enjoy each other's company.'

From that time on, he favoured me with his presence in an entirely new way. This was the most wonderful of all my graces, to judge by what it has always done for me. I began to see him, feel him near me, hear his voice—spiritual impressions, which were much more vivid than any physical ones. Sense impressions could have proved distracting; as it was, there was no danger of my getting in the way, for I had no hand in these. The effect of it all was such utter self-abasement that my first impression was of being plunged into the depths of nothingness, annihilated; and so it has always remained. God's infinite greatness demands such respect and reverence from me that I've always felt I must kneel, or fall flat on my face, in his presence; in fact, I've made a habit of this ever since profession—my work and my constitution permitting. Our Lord left me no peace in any less respectful posture: he had made me so keenly aware of my extreme unworthiness that I was overcome with shame, and I'd only dare be seated if someone else was present. I longed to be forgotten, or at least only to meet with scorn, humiliations and insults; after all, that's all I deserve. Jesus, my only Love, agreed to this —so much so that, in spite of being proud and sensitive, I could only find satisfaction in being thwarted, humbled and abased. This, he had made up his mind, was to be my delicious spiritual food; and he has never let me run short of it, nor complain that I've had enough. If ever I allowed myself to go without it, or those around me failed to provide it, our Lord took it on himself to supply me with something to keep me going. Whenever he had a hand in it, however, I used to feel things much more keenly. . . . But it would prove too tiresome, if I put all this into words.

He began to favour me now with visits under various disguises: sometimes he would be a dear friend, sometimes the fondest of bridegrooms, sometimes a father wrapped up in his only child; and so on. But I'm keeping quiet about the effect all this had on me. I'll only tell you that he showed me his twofold holiness—the holiness of love and the holiness of justice. Each was absolute in its own right, and I was constantly under the influence of both. The holiness of God's love had me suffering a kind of purgatory, very painful to endure; I was being given a chance to relieve the sufferings of those holy souls actually in purgatory whom God would allow to turn to me for help. As for the holiness of his justice —I felt the full weight of its severity. It is appalling and dreadful, where sinners are concerned, and I was being made to suffer for them—'especially,' our Lord told me, 'for those who are dedicated to me; later on, I shall reveal, and let you experience, the sufferings which my love will ask you to bear for their sakes.'

CHAPTER VIII

THE DIVINE DIRECTOR

Y O U know how ignorant I am, my God. You know I can't find words to describe what has happened since— all the workings of your love and grace, the whole relationship between your royal majesty and your unworthy, puny slave. Give me some way of describing just a little of it all, the bit that is evident and most easily understood. It will help to show how prodigal your love has made you to one who is so wretched and of such little worth.

I'd no secrets where my Superior and Novice-mistress were concerned, even though quite often I didn't understand what I was telling them. Extraordinary ways, they'd made me realise, were out of place in the Holy Marys; and this left me very upset. I tried every means of avoiding that sort of thing, but it was no use; it had got such a hold over me, I couldn't control it any longer. It was the same with my other faculties— they seemed to be completely absorbed. I made every effort to keep to the method of mental prayer taught me along with the other exercises; but nothing would stay in my mind for long. My points for meditation nicely read—they would all evaporate! The only things I could learn and remember were what my divine Master taught me; but as my superiors were doing everything they could to undo the work he was doing, and told me to do the same, I had a lot to suffer. I did my best to put up a fight, scrupulously obedient down to the least detail in doing what I was told, to free myself from our Lord's influence. But he was too strong for me.

'Royal Master,' I'd expostulate, 'why can't you let me be ordinary! Have you brought me here, to your own house, only to be the ruin of me? Keep these unusual graces for select souls, who will make better use of them and give you greater glory; I'm always being difficult. Your love and your cross will satisfy me; they will be enough to make me a good religious, and that's all I want.'

I was given my answer: 'Let us fight it out, child; I don't mind! We shall see who will come off best, the Creator or his creature, strength or weakness, omnipotence or impotence; only . . . once victory comes, whoever has it will keep it for ever.' This upset me so much that he added: 'Get this into your head: I'm not in the least offended when the fights you put up and the difficulties you make are due to obedience; I gave my life for that. But it's time you learned that I have absolute mastery over both my gifts and my creatures, and nothing can stop me from carrying out my plans. That is why you are not only to do what your superiors tell you, but you are not even to obey me without their consent. What I like is obedience, and no one can please me without it.'

My Superior was highly delighted, when she heard what he had said, and told me to surrender to his influence. This I did, and all at once the cruel oppression I'd been suffering lifted; I felt happy and at peace. Our Lord asked me, after Communion, to renew my sacrifice of myself and my freedom. I did so with all my heart, though I added: 'As long as anything unusual in your dealings with me will serve as an opportunity of greater humiliation and self-abasement, and leave everyone with a poor opinion of me. For alas, my God, I feel my weakness; I fear I may betray you, and that your gifts will not be safe with me.'

'Have no fear, my child,' he told me. 'I shall see that all goes well. I shall look after them myself and render you incapable of standing in my way.'

'Does that mean, my God, that you are going to deprive me of any suffering at all?'

Immediately, I was shown a large cross—so big, I couldn't see the top of it—but it was covered with flowers. 'That's the marriage-bed of my chaste brides,' he said. 'There we shall share, you and I, the delights of my pure love. Little by little these flowers will fall; only the thorns will remain—the thorns they are hiding as yet on account of your weakness. They will prick you, those thorns; and you'll feel the pain so keenly, you will need all the strength my love can give you in order to bear it.'

These words made me very happy. There could never be enough suffering, I thought, never enough of humiliation or contempt—at least, not enough to quench the burning thirst I had for it. Lack of suffering seemed to me to be the biggest suffering of all, for God's love left me no peace, day or night. But these delights disturbed me; all I wanted was the cross, nothing else. I'd have been glad to find myself overburdened with austerities and work; and indeed, I went as far as my strength would let me, for I couldn't live without suffering— even for an instant. The greater my sufferings, the better I satisfied the holiness of God's love, which had me longing desperately for three things: suffering, holy Communion to increase my love, and death to make me one with him.

It didn't seem to matter what they did with me now; I didn't care about time or place any longer—my royal Master was my constant companion. He'd given himself to me, I knew, because he is so good and not because I'm in the least deserving of it. This meant that no one could take him from me, and so I was happy anywhere. It was my experience during the retreat I had to make before my profession. . . . I was told to look after an ass and its tiny foal in the garden. I had my hands full, and no mistake! I wasn't allowed to tie them up, but told to see that they stayed in one little corner, in case they did any damage. As they did nothing but scamper about, I hadn't a moment's peace until the evening *Angelus*, when I went in to supper. Later, during Matins, I'd go back to the stable and feed them. I was so happy doing this, it could have lasted a lifetime, for all I cared; my royal Master was such a faithful companion, I was never distracted by all the running about I had to do.

That was a time of wonderful graces for me; never have I known anything like them. There was one in particular, when he gave me an insight into the mystery of his passion and death. . . . but it's too deep to write about, and too long, so I must leave it out. I'll only say that it gave me such a love for the cross, I couldn't live for a moment without suffering; but I had to suffer in silence, doing without consolation, comfort or pity, and sharing my Master's death, crushed under the weight of a cross—calumny, grief, humiliation, neglect and scorn of every kind. That's the way in which God, mercifully, has let me spend my whole life—doing such things which are expressions of pure love. He has never stinted these dishes, in which he takes an epicure's delight, always taking good care to keep me well supplied with them. He never says: 'That's enough!'

Once, after I'd done something wrong, my divine Master had this lesson for me: 'I am a holy Master,' he told me, 'and I teach holiness. I am pure, and I cannot bear the least stain. That is why simplicity must colour everything you do, letting me see that your motives are right and pure; for I cannot bear the slightest subterfuge. You will learn—I shall see to it—that, although I have become your Master because I love you so much, and in order to teach you and fashion you to my liking for the purpose I have in view, still I cannot bear half-hearted or cowardly souls. Although I am kindly in putting up with your weakness, you will find me no less stern and strict in correcting and punishing you, should you prove unfaithful.' He has let me feel this all my life. Not even the smallest fault was allowed to pass, I can tell you, however little deliberation or carelessness I might plead. He never failed to call me to order, and punish me—so mercifully and kindly all the same.

Still, I must admit that nothing used to hurt me more dread-fully than to know that he was even ever so slightly displeased with me; no other suffering, correction or mortification was anything like this. It used to have me running off then and there to beg a penance for my fault—for only a penance covered by obedience would please our Lord. His sternest reprimands were reserved for want of respect and attention in the presence of the Blessed Sacrament (especially during Office and mental prayer), insincerity or failure to preserve purity of intention, and idle curiosity. The tiniest deficiency in the matter of charity or humility is visible to his pure and penetrating gaze, and also earns a severe scolding. But this is nothing compared with failures to obey superiors or the rules! The slightest syllable indicative of unwillingness is something he simply cannot stand from the lips of a religious. 'You're deceiving yourself,' he told me, 'if you think that behaviour or mortifications dictated by self-will can in any way appeal to me. Self-will would bend superiors to its own way sooner than give it up. Rotten fruit—that's all it is; and I'll have you know, I won't touch it. Self-will horrifies me in a religious; I'd rather she took every little relaxation which obedience offers than load herself with austerities and fastings of her own choice.'

Whenever I happen to carry out such self-imposed mortifications and penances, unasked for by our Lord or my Superior, he won't even let me offer them to him. Instead, he corrects me with a penance of his own choosing. All my shortcomings are met in this way, and each has its own special punishment in the purgatory where he purifies me, so that I am less unworthy of his presence, his message, and his power at work in me—for he is responsible for everything I do. Once, after I had taken the discipline for the space of an *Ave Maris Stella*, as I'd been told to do, he said: 'That's for me.' But as I still carried on, he added: 'That, now, is for the devil! . . .' I couldn't stop quickly enough. Another time I was taking it for the holy souls in purgatory: and as I made to go on longer than I had permission for, they were all around me complaining that I was hitting them. At this, I resolved to die rather than overstep, by ever so little, the bounds of obedience; and afterwards our Lord had me doing penance for my fault.

But nothing seemed difficult to me in those days. He was still keeping the full severity of my trials and sufferings lost in the sweetness of his love. Time and again I'd beg him to leave me, so as to let me enjoy to the full the bitter-sweet experience of his anguish, loneliness, agony, shame, and other sufferings. But he used to tell me that my business was simply to fit in unconcernedly with all his plans; it wasn't my place to dictate to him at all! 'I'll show you later,' he added, 'that I am a wise and learned Director. I can lead souls safely, whenever —self-forgetting—they leave themselves entirely in my hands.'

CHAPTER IX

REVELATIONS

I WAS given so much work to do, it left me scarcely any spare time. Once,[1] however, when I happened to have a little more time to myself than usual, and I was spending it in front of the Blessed Sacrament, God's presence seemed to envelop me completely. I forgot all about myself, and where I was, it was so intense; I simply gave myself up to the Spirit of God—my heart, a willing prey to the violence of his love. For a long time he kept me leaning on his breast, while he revealed the wonders of his love and the mysterious secrets of his sacred Heart. Till then, he had always kept them hidden; but now, for the first time, he opened his Heart to me. The realistic and tangible way in which he did so, as well as the effects which this grace had on me, left no room for any doubt; still, I'm always afraid of being mistaken whenever I describe what goes on inside me. What happened, I think, was this. . . .

'My divine Heart,' he told me, 'is so passionately fond of the human race, and of you in particular, that it cannot keep back the pent-up flames of its burning charity any longer. They must burst out through you and reveal my Heart to the world, so as to enrich mankind with my precious treasures. I'm letting you see them now; and they include all the graces of sanctification and salvation needed to snatch men from the very brink of hell. You are the one I have chosen for this

[1] 27 December 1673.

44

great scheme—you're so utterly unworthy and ignorant, it will be all *my* work.'

Next, he asked me for my heart. I begged him to take it; he did, and placed it in his own divine Heart. He let me see it there—a tiny atom being completely burned up in that fiery furnace. Then, lifting it out—now a little heart-shaped flame—he put it back where he had found it. 'There, my well-beloved,' I heard him saying, 'that's a precious proof of my love for you, hiding in your side a little spark from its hottest flames. That will be your heart from now on; it will burn you up—to your very last breath; its intense heat will never diminish—only blood-letting will cool it slightly. But I shall cast the shadow of my cross over your bleeding; so deeply, it will bring you more humiliation and suffering than relief. That is why I insist that you ask for this treatment in all simplicity; you will then be doing what you are told,[1] as well as finding satisfaction in shedding your blood on the cross of humiliation. As a proof that the great grace I have just given you is not an illusion, but the basis of all those which I have still in store for you . . . although I've closed the wound in your side, you will always feel the pain of it. And how have you been describing yourself up to the present: my slave? Well, now I'm giving you a new name: the beloved disciple of my sacred Heart.'

What a great favour all this was! While it lasted—such a long time—I didn't know where I was . . . heaven or earth, it was all the same to me. For several days afterwards, it was as though I were all on fire and intoxicated. Only by an immense effort could I bring myself round to utter a single word, I was so completely beside myself. So tremendous was the effort needed to go to recreation or to eat anything, it was almost too much for me—a cause of deep humiliation. And I couldn't sleep; this wound in my side—though I wouldn't exchange its pain for anything—becomes so intensely hot, it

---

[1] The Visitation nuns are recommended by their Constitution to ask the Superior trustfully for anything they may think they need.

eats me up and roasts me alive. I felt so saturated with God, I just couldn't explain myself to my Superior as I'd have liked to have done. Because of the sorrow and shame I always experience in telling of these graces—owing to my unworthiness—I'd far rather have told everybody my sins. It would have been such a consolation, if only they had let me do that—let me read my general confession out loud in the refectory. Once shown the depths of my depravity, no one could have ascribed to any merits of mine the graces I was receiving.

On the first Friday of each month there was a repetition of the favour to which I referred when talking about the pain in my side. This is what used to happen: I'd see the Sacred Heart like a dazzling sun, its burning rays shining right into my heart—setting it ablaze so fiercely, I'd keep thinking I was going to be reduced to ashes. My divine Master used to take special advantage of these occasions, to teach me his plans for me, and to let me into the secrets of his loving Heart. One, from many, stands out. . . .

The Blessed Sacrament was exposed, and I was experiencing an unusually complete state of recollection, my senses and faculties utterly withdrawn from their surroundings, when Jesus Christ, my kind Master, appeared to me. He was a blaze of glory—his five wounds shining like five suns, flames issuing from all parts of his human form, especially from his divine breast which was like a furnace, and which he opened to disclose his utterly affectionate and lovable heart, the living source of all those flames. It was at this moment that he revealed to me the indescribable wonders of his pure love for mankind: the extravagance to which he'd been led for those who had nothing for him but ingratitude and indifference. 'This hurts me more,' he told me, 'than everything I suffered in my passion. Even a little love from them in return—and I should regard all that I have done for them as next to nothing, and look for a way of doing still more. But no; all my eager efforts for their welfare meet with nothing but coldness and dislike. Do me the kindness, then—you, at least—of making up for all their ingratitude, as far as you can.' When I pointed out my incapacity, he replied: ' Here you are! This will make good your deficiencies, every one of them! ' His divine Heart opening as he spoke, such a scorching flame shot forth as I was sure would devour me. It went right through me; and when I could bear it no longer I begged him to take pity on my weakness.

' I shall be your support,' he told me; ' don't be afraid. Simply focus all your attention on my voice—on what I am asking of you so as to fit you for the fulfilment of my plans. First of all, you are to receive me in the holy Eucharist as often as obedience allows. Accept any mortification or humiliation that may result, as a token of my love. Besides this, you are to receive Communion on the first Friday of each month. Then, every Thursday night, I shall give you a share in that fatal sadness which I allowed myself to feel in the garden of olives; death couldn't be so hard as the agonised state to which this sadness will reduce you. You are to get up between eleven o'clock and midnight, to keep me company in humble prayer to my Father, exactly as I spent that night of my agony. Lie face downwards with me for an hour—not only to allay God's anger by asking mercy for sinners, but also to soothe in some way the heartache I felt when my apostles deserted me, when I had to reproach them for being unable to watch with me even for an hour.* And, during this hour, you are to do what I show you. But listen, child! Don't believe lightly in every inspiration, and don't be too sure of it—Satan is furiously bent on deceiving you. So don't do anything without the approval of those who are guiding you. As long as you have the sanction of obedience, he can never delude you; he is completely power- less over those who obey.'

I lost consciousness for the entire duration of the vision I've just described; and when they came to take me away, I had no idea where I was. As they couldn't get any answers out of me, and as I had the greatest difficulty in standing on my feet, they

E

took me to our Mother.[1] At the sight of me there in front of her, apparently out of my wits, all hot and trembling, and sinking to my knees, she tried every way she knew to mortify and humiliate me. This was a pleasure, as far as I was concerned, and it filled me with unbelievable happiness; I seemed such a shameful creature in my own eyes, I'd have felt that even the harshest treatment was too mild. I stood there, covered with confusion, and told her what had happened. After I'd finished, she set about humiliating me more than ever. For once, she wouldn't allow me to do any of the things I believed our Lord was asking me to do; she simply ridiculed my whole story. This cheered me up immensely, and I took myself off very much at peace.

As a result of the fire consuming me, I fell into a violent fever which showed no signs of abating. I was too delighted with the suffering, to complain about it; in fact, I didn't mention it at all until my strength gave out. The doctor's diagnosis confirmed that the fever was of long-standing, and I endured more than sixty bouts of it altogether.* Never have I felt so relieved! My burning thirst for suffering was being quenched to some extent by the excessive pain throughout my body. Only the wood of the cross—suffering, scorn, humiliation and pain of every kind—could feed and satisfy that devouring fire; and never have I known any pain to equal the agony I felt in not suffering enough—it quite looked as though I would die of it.

Our Lord still kept bestowing graces on me, however. The most wonderful one came during a fainting-fit, when it seemed as though the three Persons of the Blessed Trinity appeared to me and filled me with indescribable happiness. I'm unable to put into words what actually happened. . . . All I can say is that the eternal Father was holding out a huge cross; it bristled with thorns and was surrounded by the other instruments of the passion. 'Look, my child!' he was saying to me; 'I am giving you the same present as I gave my well-beloved

[1] Mother de Saumaise.

Son.' Then Jesus Christ, my Lord, added: 'And I shall fasten you to the cross as I was fastened to it, and I'll keep you constant company there.' The third of these divine Persons went on to tell me: 'I am Love; as you are purified on the cross, I shall consume you.' It is impossible to imagine the peace and happiness which flooded my soul; and the impression left by these divine Persons has never grown dim. They looked like three young men; they were dressed in white, brilliantly illuminated, equally handsome, and of the same age and height. I didn't understand the full import of this vision at the time, as I have come to later on—the severe sufferings in store for me.

When my superiors told me to ask our Lord to make me well again, I did so; but I was afraid lest my prayer be answered. If my health were restored, however, then they'd be convinced—they told me—that it really was God at work in me. Once they were sure of that, they'd let me carry out his instructions—both as regards going to Communion on the first Fridays and watching for an hour every Thursday night. After I'd conveyed all this to our Lord, under obedience, I immediately recovered my health. It happened this way. . . .

I was privileged with a vision of the blessed Virgin, my good Mother. She was extremely affectionate, and talked to me for quite a long time. 'Take heart, dear child,' were her last words. 'My divine Son asked me, on his behalf, to give you back your health. You still have a long and difficult way to go, always on the cross, pierced by nails and thorns, and torn with scourges. But there's nothing to be afraid of; I'll never leave you—and I promise you, you can rely on my protection.'

She has often let me feel the truth of that promise since, when I have been in real need of it.

CHAPTER X

TWO PORTRAITS—
THE DEVIL ATTACKS

M Y royal Lord continued favouring me with his
presence the whole time. It was a presence I could
really feel, as I said before; and he had promised it
would last for ever. Sure enough, even when I've done something wrong, he hasn't withdrawn it. His holiness, however,
cannot tolerate the least stain. He has pointed out to me even
the smallest imperfection; he couldn't stand the slightest trace
of anything like that, even though I'd only been the tiniest bit
wilful or careless. Since I'm so wretchedly imperfect, I commit
a lot of faults although I don't mean to; and to be in the
presence of that holiness, when I've let myself be unfaithful,
is, I confess, more than I can bear. I'd cheerfully go through
any kind of torture rather than endure the presence of this
holy God with the least stain of sin on my soul. I'd prefer to
plunge into a furnace—it would be far less agonising!

Once I gave way to a trace of vanity in speaking of myself.
. . . Only God knows the tears and groans this fault cost
me. For, when we were alone together, with a severe look on
his face he called me to order : 'What have you to boast of,
dust and ashes? You are nothing, wretched; never forget that,
and don't try to climb above your station. To prevent the
greatness of my gifts from leading you to misread yourself
and forget of what stuff you are made, I intend to let you
see a picture of yourself.' There and then he unfolded that

50

repulsive portrait before my eyes—an epitome of every facet of my being. I was so shocked and horrified, I'd have fainted for grief if he hadn't sustained me. Unable to stand the sight of myself, I felt that his amazing goodness and mercy in putting up with me, in not already plunging me into hell, just didn't make sense.

That was how he punished me for the tiniest sparks of vanity. Sometimes I was forced to exclaim: 'Alas, my God, either let me die, or hide this picture; I cannot look at it and live!' He had me hating myself until I couldn't stand it any longer; and as obedience wouldn't let me carry out the strict measures all this urged me to take with myself, I can't describe what I had to go through. I knew, of course, that my royal Master was satisfied with everything obedience had me doing; but what used to please him most was to see me humiliated. So I never failed to accuse myself of my faults; the hardest penance this could bring me would still be easier than one from our Lord himself—and he saw faults where you'd think no fault could be found.

He brought this home to me one All Saints' Day, when I distinctly heard a voice saying:

> 'Innocence can brook no dross;
> Power bolts the door to loss;
> Nothing fades in bliss above—
> Everything enriched by love.'

I was also told the meaning of these words, and it's given me plenty of food for thought for some time. 'Innocence can brook no dross'—this meant that I was not to endure the slightest stain on my soul. 'Power bolts the door to loss'—this meant that I had to leave myself completely in our Lord's hands; he was power itself, and we'd have nothing to lose if we gave him everything. The other lines—they referred to paradise, where nothing passes away; everything is eternal there, where love reigns over all. I was even given a tiny foretaste of that glory. . . . God bless me, what a thrill of joy and longing filled my heart! In retreat at the time, I spent the whole day enjoying things which beggar description. There seemed to be nothing to prevent me from going to heaven there and then—until I heard the voice again, and learned how far out I was.

'Vainly sighs your heart, desiring
Speedy entrance there;
Every soul to bliss aspiring
Calvary's way must fare.'

Then followed a picture of everything I should have to suffer all through my life, and I shuddered from head to toe; . . . though, at the time, I didn't grasp all the implications of this picture as fully as ensuing events disclosed them.

I was preparing to make my annual confession, and very worried in trying to discover my sins, when my divine Master remarked: 'Why are you torturing yourself? Do what you can; I'll make good whatever may be wanting. A heart that is humbled and contrite—that's all I ask in this sacrament; a heart sincerely resolved not to offend me again, open in self-accusation. Such a heart will never find me slow to pardon, and perfect amendment follows.'

God's influence was at work in me, independently of my own efforts. So completely did it dominate body and soul, no joy or sadness could fill my heart but what he wanted, no thoughts enter my mind but those he sent. This has always given me a queer feeling of being deceived, despite every possible assurance to the contrary—not only from God, but from the guidance of my superiors. Any spiritual directors I've had were there for the purpose of examining the way God was leading me; he gave them perfect freedom to approve or disapprove of it. The trouble was that, instead of pulling me out of the deluded state in which I really believed myself to be, they only plunged me deeper into it—my confessors and others

—by telling me to surrender to his influence! I was to submit unreservedly to his guidance, and never fail to follow his inspirations—even though I thought I was being turned into the devil's plaything.

Well, I made my annual confession. Afterwards, I had the almost palpable sensation of being undressed and reclothed at once in a white robe. I could also hear these words: 'Here it is, the robe of innocence! I am clothing your soul in it, so that your life may be a prolongation of my Incarnation. You will go on living, I mean, but it will not be with your own life any longer; I shall be living in you. I am your life; for the future you will only live because of me. Your activities I mean to be my activities; you are to let me work through you, leaving the care of everything to me. No longer are you to have a will of your own, but let me do the willing for you—always and everywhere.'

Then, there was the time my only Love appeared to me and held out two pictures, one in each hand. One of them portrayed a life of happiness greater than a religious could dream of— complete peace, inward and outward consolations, perfect health, together with human approval or esteem and similar naturally pleasing things. The other portrait showed a life of poverty and abasement—a constant crucifixion by means of every kind of humiliation, frustration and contempt, with continuous sufferings in body and mind. 'Choose, my child!' he said, putting them in front of me. 'Choose the one you would like to have. The same graces will follow whichever one you choose.' Throwing myself at his feet in adoration, I replied: 'Lord: you are all I want; I leave the choice to you.' As he still went on pressing me to choose, I repeated my protests: 'My God, you are all I need to make me happy. You choose the one that will bring you the greater glory, and don't consider my likes or feelings at all. Please yourself, and I shall be satisfied.' He told me then that, like Mary Magdalen, I had chosen the best part of all, which would never be taken away from me, since it was to be my portion for ever. 'There you are! ' he said, offering me the crucifixion picture. ' That's my choice for you, that's what I like best—it will fulfil my plans and it will also make you more like me. The other picture is of the life of bliss reserved for heaven: it leaves no opportunity for merit.'

So I took the picture of death and crucifixion, kissing the hand that gave it; and even though from the natural point of view that portrait made me shudder, I embraced it with all my love. As I clasped it to my heart, it seemed to leave its mark on me to such an extent that I felt I was just a medley now of everything I had seen in it. I underwent so great a change, I didn't know what was happening. Still, I left everything to my Superior's judgment. I couldn't hide anything from her, and neither could I omit to carry out any order she gave me—so long as it came direct from her. The divine influence which I experienced led to a terrible reluctance on my part whenever she ordered me to do something on the advice of others, or to be guided by them. . . . You see, our Lord had promised me that he would always see that she had enough light to guide me along the way he wanted me to go.

It was during holy Communion and at night that God, in his goodness, would give me his greatest graces. On Thursday nights especially, I used to receive indescribable favours. Because of this, our Lord warned me once that Satan had asked permission to try me like gold in the crucible of contradictions, humiliations, temptations, and make me feel utterly forsaken. Permission had been given—except that I was not to be tempted against purity.[1] Our Lord wouldn't allow the devil to make any difficulties for me on that score; he hadn't even allowed the faintest trace of it in his own case, he hated the vice so much. As for all other temptations, however, I'd have to be on my guard—pride, despair and gluttony were the ones to watch out for most of all. I was more frightened of all this than I was of death, but our Lord assured me that

---

[1] There was one exception; cf. p. 75, where she describes a temptation of this sort which she once had to face.

there was really nothing to fear. He'd be deep down inside me, so that nothing could touch me; he'd be fighting for me, and I'd find in him the reward of my victories; he'd enfold me with his power, for fear I gave way to the attacks. I was to be continually on the alert, he added, especially for attacks from the outside; he'd look after the inside himself.

I hadn't long to wait before I heard my tormentor threatening me. He looked like some hideous Arab: his eyes were blazing coals, and he was grinding his teeth. 'Damned soul!' he spat. 'I'll have you yet; and once I manage to get you in my clutches, I'll show you! I'll hurt you everywhere.' But all these threats, and more besides, left me quite unmoved—I could feel such inward reserves of strength. All hell's fury would have found me unafraid, I'm sure; for—besides this inner strength —I had a little crucifix to which my royal Redeemer had attached the power of warding off all such diabolical assaults. Day and night I wore it next my heart; and it was a great help to me.

I was sent to help in the infirmary. God alone knows all I had to suffer there, due to my quick, sensitive nature—to say nothing of other people and the devil. It was quite common for the devil to make me fall and break whatever I was carrying. He'd taunt me then, sometimes laughing in my face: 'Clumsy one! You'll never be any use!' This left me so sad and miserable, I didn't know what to do; and he'd frequently make it impossible for me to confide in our Mother—obedience pulled him up short and weakened his hold. Once, when I was carrying a pan of red-hot coals, he pushed me from the top of the stairs. I was quite unscathed when I reached the bottom, and the coals were still in the pan; but those who saw me fall were sure I'd broken my legs. However, I'd been conscious of my guardian angel supporting me.

I had the happiness of seeing him many a time, this angel of mine, and often he'd find fault with me and correct me. There was the time when I was about to involve myself in a discussion over the marriage of one of my relatives. . . . My good angel reprimanded me severely, and let me see that such behaviour was unworthy of a religious. If ever I took part in that sort of gossip again, he said, he wouldn't let me see him any more. The least want of modesty or respect in the presence of my royal Master was something the angel simply couldn't tolerate. I'd see him bow down to the ground in humble reverence, and he'd want me to do the same. Whenever possible, I did so—no other position could have been more of a relief in my continued mental and physical sufferings: it corresponded to that nothingness of mine in which I was always conscious of being swallowed up, not only in what I had to suffer, but even in the delights I experienced—delights I could never enjoy.

CHAPTER XI

VICTIM SOUL

THE holiness of God's love was demanding something in return—its tribute of suffering. So insistent was it, I couldn't feel perfectly at ease unless I was experiencing physical pain or mental anguish, unless I was utterly humiliated, despised and contradicted. I never went short of all that sort of thing, even for a moment—God's grace saw to that; if suffering didn't come from outside, it came from within. Whenever my stocks of this healthy diet began to dwindle, he'd urge me to look for more in the way of mortification—and my sensitive, proud temperament kept me supplied with plenty of material. He was determined that I shouldn't lose a single opportunity; and if I did happen to miss one (it used to cost me a great effort to overcome my dislikes), he made sure that I paid double for it.

When he wanted anything from me, he'd be so insistent that I just couldn't refuse. (This meant that I had a lot to endure; I often wanted to resist, as he led me by paths I naturally disliked—he wouldn't have me travel any other way . . . ever.) So dainty was I, the slightest uncleanliness used to turn my stomach. Our Lord took such a strict line with me over this that once I set about cleaning up an invalid's vomit with unnecessary thoroughness.* 'Had I a thousand bodies, a thousand loves, a thousand lives, I should immolate them in your service,' I told him. I found such happiness in what I had done, I'd have been glad to meet with similar opportunities every day—lessons in self-conquest, seen only by God. Though

57

I couldn't have done it without the strength which he was good enough to give me, he left me in no doubt that he was pleased. It was the following night, if I'm not mistaken . . . for two or three hours he kept my lips pressed close to the wound in his sacred Heart. I'd find it extremely difficult to put into words, not only what I felt on this occasion, but also the effect this grace had on me, heart and soul. But I've said enough to give you some idea of God's goodness and mercy to even a wretched creature like me.

He wouldn't let me grow less sensitive, however, nor find any escape from my intense dislikes—that was to be my tribute to what he endured in the garden of olives, and also provide me with opportunities of victory and humiliation. But the pity of it is, I'm unfaithful and often fall. Sometimes it seems as though our Lord is glad when this happens—it puts my pride in its place and makes me mistrust myself: I see that without him I can only reap a sinful harvest—a succession of falls from which I couldn't get up again. But there he was, Jesus, my only Love, ever at my call. Like a kind father, he'd hold out his loving hands to me and say: ' Now you realise that without me you cannot do anything.'* I was so grateful to him for his goodness to me, my eyes would fill with tears as I became aware that outbursts of love were his only answer to my sins and constant disloyalty. Apparently this was his way of meeting my lack of response to grace—something he was often showing me, together with his many graces, so that I couldn't find any words for him, but only tears. I suffered more than I can tell. That's how this divine Lover amused himself with his unworthy slave.

Nursing another patient, once, also turned my stomach. Our Lord reprimanded me so sternly, I felt driven—while carrying away a pan she had used—to put my lips to it in reparation. I'd have swallowed what she left in it, if he hadn't reminded me of the rule about not eating without permission.* ' You're mad! ' he went on. ' Fancy doing a loathsome thing like that! '

'Lord,' I replied, 'I did it to please you, to win your Heart. You won't refuse me that, I hope! There are no limits to what you have done to win men's hearts, and yet they won't yield to you; often they just thrust you to one side.'

'You're right, my child. Love has had me sacrificing everything for them, and they have nothing for me in return. But I mean you to make up for their ingratitude, through the merits of my sacred Heart; for that is what I am going to give you— my Heart. Before that happens, though, you are to offer yourself as its victim and so turn aside the punishments which my Father's outraged justice has in store for a religious community —calling in his just anger for their correction.'

The community, the defects which annoyed him, and everything I was to suffer in soothing his righteous wrath—I saw them all, then and there. My whole being shuddered, and I hadn't the courage to sacrifice myself. As I wasn't my own mistress, I told him, I couldn't do it without the permission of my superiors. I was so afraid I'd be made to do it, however, that I kept putting off mentioning it to them. But our Lord was forever at my heels; he gave me no peace at all, and I'd frequently burst into tears. There was nothing for it, in the end, but to tell my Superior.[1] Though my distress was only too obvious, she told me to sacrifice myself unreservedly to all God's demands. This simply had me in a worse state than ever —I just couldn't pluck up enough courage to agree, and went on being difficult.

On the day before the feast of the Presentation,[2] however, I had a vision. I saw God's justice, which seemed so terrible in its formidable battle array, I was frightened out of my wits. Like St Paul, I felt paralysed, as I heard a voice saying: 'This is a thankless task of yours, kicking against the goad of my justice! Since you've done all you could to avoid the humiliations which this sacrifice would cause you, I'm going to give you twice as many. I was only asking for a hidden sacrifice;

---

[1] Mother de Saumaise.
[2] 20 November 1677.

now, I intend it to be public. What it will be like, and when it will happen—that's beyond all human calculation. But the circumstances will be so humiliating as to be a source of shame to you—in your own eyes and before others—for the rest of your life. You'll understand, then, what it means to resist God!'

Sure enough, I learned the lesson! I'd never known myself in such a state. I'll tell you a little of what happened—but not everything! It was after the evening meditation . . . all the others left the choir, but I couldn't move; there I stayed, sobbing and groaning, until the last bell for supper. I went off to take my collation (it was the eve of the Presentation), dragging myself by a superhuman effort of will to the community room. There, I felt impelled to make my sacrifice out loud in the way God had given me to understand that he wanted it done. This meant that I had to go and see my Superior, who was ill at the time. I must admit, however, that I was so distraught, I felt like someone bound hand and foot; all I could do was cry—which I did copiously—and it seemed to be the only indication I could give of what I was going through. The most degraded of criminals—that's how I saw myself—being dragged by ropes to the place of execution. I saw God's holiness, armed with the thunderbolts of his just anger, about to hurl them at me. It looked as though I'd be swallowed up by the gaping jaws of hell, which I could see opening to engulf me. I felt I was being consumed by fire right down to the marrow of my bones, and a curious quaking sensation caused me to shiver all over. All I could say was: 'Have mercy on me, O God, as thou art ever rich in mercy!'[1] Groaning under the weight of all this anguish, I couldn't reach my Superior's room until, about eight o'clock, one of our Sisters found me and took me along. Mother Superior was quite surprised to see the state I was in. I couldn't put my case at all—though I falsely imagined, to add to my sufferings, that it was immediately obvious to everyone—but she knew the

[1] Psalm 50.

influence obedience had over me, and ordered me to tell her what was troubling me. At once I told her about the complete and utter sacrifice of myself which God wanted me to make in front of the whole community. I also told her the reason why he was asking it, though I won't mention it here for fear of offending against charity. (This would wound the Heart of Jesus, charity's source—and he won't hear of any excuses for damaging that precious virtue.)

Well, I did it in the end, the thing my royal Master wanted. There was a good deal of talk, and the community's reactions in speech and thought were varied—but I'm leaving all that to the mercy of God. This I can vouch for: I don't think I have ever suffered so much. If everything I've endured before or since were put together and lasted until I die, I don't think it could equal what I went through that night—scenes of frightful confusion as they dragged me around here, there and everywhere. Our Lord was favouring me with just a tiny sample of the agonies which he experienced during the night of his passion.

Noisily and sleeplessly my night of anguish (and God alone knows what it was like) dragged by, until it was about time for Mass. Then I thought I heard these words: 'Peace is declared at last! The holiness of my justice is satisfied by your sacrifice in honour of that which I made at the moment of my Incarnation in my Mother's womb. I wanted to join the merits of my sacrifice to yours, and so renew it—with love, as I've already shown you, for our motive. Whatever you do or suffer in future, you are not to think in terms of profit to yourself—to win yourself more merit, to satisfy for your sins, or anything like that. You've given it all up for love, leaving me to apportion it where I will. You are to follow my example now, and work and suffer in silence—your one concern being to glorify God through the enthronement of my sacred Heart in the hearts of men; and I mean to reveal my Heart to them through you.'

I received these instructions after my Communion. I still

had to suffer, but I accepted this—and all the sufferings it was revealed God might have in store for me up to the day of judgment—and it brought me a sense of peace that nothing could disturb. God saw to it that I should be an object of suspicion and meet with opposition, collecting nothing but rebukes, contempt and humiliations. I'd see them pouring in on me from all sides, and yet it made me happy—in spite of the fact that I had no consolation, human or divine. I felt as though it were all one gigantic plot to crush me. . . . Their never-ending questions, the scanty answers they dragged out of me, only added to the torture. I couldn't speak, I couldn't sleep; all I could do, the only rest I could find, was to fall on my face before God. He kept on cutting me down to size, to the nonentity that I am; and I went on weeping, groaning, and pleading for mercy and relief from the thunderbolts of his just anger.

My duties in the community at that time kept me fully occupied mentally and physically. It was unbearable torture. In spite of all that I was going through, my royal Master wouldn't let me leave one of them out or ask to be excused from them; the same applied to other duties and to keeping the rule. I felt all the time as though an unseen power was dragging me to fresh scenes of torture; there was no escaping it anywhere. Suffering engulfed me and riveted all my attention; I could only think about and live for what would make me suffer. I had no option but to go the hard way—the way most distasteful to unmortified nature and my own likes and dislikes.

It was noticed that I didn't eat anything. Both my Superior and my confessor strongly reprimanded me for this, and ordered me to eat everything set before me in the refectory— an obedience which I considered beyond my strength. Our Lord, however, whose help was never wanting when I needed it, enabled me to do so without retort or excuse—though the end of each meal found me running off to bring it all up again. This went on for such a long time, it weakened my inside and caused me a great deal of pain. When they had second-thoughts about the obedience they had given me, and allowed me to eat only as much as I wanted, even that little bit I couldn't retain. Eating has been a great trial to me ever since, I must admit; going to the refectory has been like going to a torture-chamber to pay the penalty of my sins. Although I tried not to pick and choose in what I was given, I couldn't help taking what seemed to be the least appetising—that's all a poor, useless creature like myself deserves. I can manage on bread and water, I'd say to myself; anything else is luxury.

But to go back to the sorry state I was in. . . . It didn't ease up; in fact, matters became worse, more humiliating and more painful. They thought I was possessed, preyed upon by the devil; and they used to drench me with holy water, and cross themselves, and pray for the evil spirit to go away. Far from taking flight, the one I was possessed by held me tighter. ' I like holy water,' he told me, ' and I am so fond of the cross, I cannot help uniting myself intimately with those who carry it as I did, and out of love for me.' My desire for suffering burst out again more than ever. My present sufferings were like a little drop of water; they didn't quench that insatiable thirst of mine, they increased it. I think I could say, however, that there was no part of me—mental or physical—which didn't have its own particular pain. No sympathy, no comfort, came my way; and the devil was unleashing all his fury. I'd have given in time and again, but for the impression I had of an extraordinary power upholding me and withstanding all that I've just described.

In the end, my Superior—unable to make me out—told me to go to Communion and ask our Lord, under obedience, to change me back to what I was before. ' Yes, my child,' he said, as I knelt there like his little victim; ' I am the High Priest of sacrifice come to give you fresh strength to enable you to be the victim of further penalties.' He did so; and I underwent such a change, I felt as though I had just been freed from slavery. But not for long; They started telling me that it was the devil who was responsible for my experiences, and—if I

F

wasn't careful—his tricks and delusions would be the ruin of me. This was a terrible blow (all my life I'd been afraid of unintentionally deceiving myself and others), and I cried and cried. I tried everything to escape from the control of that inner influence, but to no avail. I couldn't rid myself of it, nor hinder its activity, in the slightest. All the powers of my soul were in its grip. I felt as though I were in a bottomless pit; and the harder I tried to get out, the deeper I seemed to sink. I tried every way they told me, but it was no use. Sometimes my struggles were so great, I'd be utterly exhausted.

My royal Master was delighted; he cheered me up so much, he calmed all my fears at once. 'What have you to be afraid of in my almighty arms?' he asked. 'From babyhood on I have been your Father, your Master, your Director; I've given you continual proofs of the loving tenderness of my divine Heart—your home in time and eternity; could I really let you perish by leaving you at the mercy of your enemies? If it will set your mind at rest, tell me what greater proof of my love you would like, and I'll give it to you. Why struggle against me? I am the one and only Friend you have.'

These reproaches made me so sorry and ashamed at my lack of trust, I determined to have nothing further to do with testing the influence I was under. I'd simply leave myself humbly and cheerfully in the hands of those around me.

CHAPTER XII

THESE THREE HEARTS

M Y Lord and my God, you are the only one who knows what an effort it is for me to rise above the reluctance and shame of writing all this, and how painful I find it to obey. Let me die rather than put down anything which you haven't truly inspired—for your glory and my shame. For pity's sake, good Jesus, never let anyone else see these pages; they are only for that one person whom you mean to go through them.[1] I don't want this manuscript to become an obstacle to my permanent burial from human memory and esteem. Please, God, give your poor, paltry slave this solace! . . . Scarcely is my plea expressed, I am being given my answer: 'Leave it all in my hands. Leave the fulfilment of my plans to me, and don't interfere; I will take care of everything.' . . . I am going through with it, then, out of obedience. I've only one aim, my God, and that is to please you by doing what, in my case, amounts almost to martyrdom. I find each word I write a sacrifice—may they always bring you glory!

God has left me in no doubt that he intends me to write this book. . . . I am attracted to my royal Master for his sake, not for what I can get out of it; I love him for himself alone. I've never clung to what he has given me, great though his gifts have been; their only value—for me—lies in the fact that they came from him. I haven't really thought about them

[1] Probably a reference to Fr Francis Rolin, S.J., who asked St Margaret Mary to write this account of her life.

much—he was the only one I had in mind; anything else means nothing to me, apart from him, so I try to forget it. Well, when it came to carrying out this obedience, I thought I'd find it impossible to write about things which happened so long ago. Our Lord has given me clear proof to the contrary; he's made it easy for me by letting me feel over again what I experienced in the events I mention. That's why I'm sure that this is what he wants.

All through the pains and fears I had to endure, I knew a constant feeling of immutable peace. Some theologians I was forced to talk to, far from dispelling my fears, only aggravated the difficulties; but, in the end, our Lord sent Father Claude de la Colombière back here.[1] He was the priest I spoke to at the start of it all.[2] . . . Shortly after consecrating myself to my royal Master, I was promised one of his servants: I was to reveal to that person all the treasures of our Lord's sacred Heart as far as I knew them, all the secrets entrusted to me. Our Lord was sending me this priest to set my mind at rest regarding the path I was travelling; and also to give the good man, during our interviews, innumerable special graces from his sacred Heart. While the reverend father was speaking to the Community, on his first visit, I heard an inner voice whisper: ' Here he is—the one I am sending you! '

I realised the truth of this the first time he heard my confession during the Ember days.[3] We'd never seen or spoken to each other before; yet he kept me a long time and seemed, from the way he spoke, to understand what was happening to me. On that occasion, however, I'd no intention of opening my heart to him. He could see that I wanted to get away, afraid of keeping the rest of the Community waiting, so he asked me if I'd like to come back to the confessional and talk to him some other time.* I wasn't my own mistress, I told him; I had to do what I was told. (My timid disposition made me

[1] In 1679.
[2] In 1675.
[3] In the Lent of 1675.

shrink from communications of this kind.) I left the confessional then, after being there nearly an hour and a half.

A little while later, he was back again. When it was my turn to go in to him, I still felt terribly reluctant to talk about myself, though I knew it was God's will. I blurted this out to begin with—only to receive the reply that he was very glad to be giving me the chance of making a sacrifice to God. Without any more ado, I calmly opened my heart to him and utterly laid bare my soul, good as well as bad. He was most encouraging, and assured me that I had nothing to fear, since the influence I experienced was never any obstacle to obedience. I was to follow its inspirations, he told me, giving myself up to it completely, offering myself as a victim when required. He was struck, it seemed, by God's goodness in being undismayed when I proved so difficult. He taught me to value God's gifts and to receive humbly and respectfully the favours of such frequent intimate revelations; I ought never to stop thanking God for being so good to me.

My royal Master never left my side, no matter where I was or what I was doing, so that I just couldn't say any vocal prayers. In spite of tremendous efforts—during the rosary especially—I'd wait, mouth open, but not a sound would come out. When I hinted at this to Father Claude, he told me not to force myself; I was to stick to the prayers laid down, and add the rosary when I could. I told him a little about the more outstanding favours I had from my Beloved, and of our loving union—things I'm not describing here—and he said that all this gave me plenty of scope for self-humiliation; as for himself, he had all the more reason for astonishment at God's great mercies to me.

God in his goodness, however, had no intention of affording me encouragement, unless I paid for it by humiliations. This interview with Father de la Colombière brought me quite a number, and the good priest himself had much to suffer on my account. The tale went round that I meant to take him in with my delusions, and lead him up the garden path as I had the others. But he didn't let that worry him; he continued to help me during his short stay in the town, and has gone on doing so ever since. I've been surprised, over and over again, that he never gave me up as the others did—the way I treated him would have put anyone else off completely. No stint, however, of humiliations and mortifications for me—he made sure of that—and it suited me down to the ground!

He was given unusual graces on one occasion, when he came to say Mass in our church; and the same thing happened to me. As I went up to make my Communion, our Lord showed me his sacred Heart—a fiery furnace in which two other hearts were becoming fused and absorbed. 'You are watching my chaste love,' he told me, 'joining these three hearts into one for all time.' This union, he made it clear to me later, was to give glory to his sacred Heart. He intended me to reveal the treasures of that Heart to the good Father, for him to make them known and preach their value and utility; and so he wanted us to be like brother and sister, sharing these spiritual favours between us. I reminded him, then, what a sorry thing I am—there could be nothing in common between a man of such great virtue and ability and a paltry little sinner like myself. 'The infinite riches of my Heart will make up for that,' our Lord replied, 'and even everything out. Just tell him this, and don't be afraid.'

At our very next interview I did as our Lord said. The humble and grateful way in which the priest received this announcement, and several other messages which our Lord had asked me to give him, touched me deeply. No amount of sermons could have done me more good. I also mentioned that our Lord had only given me these graces so that I could pass them on to others who would give him glory. . . . I was to do this by either speech or pen, as our Lord would indicate. I was not to worry about how to say or write these things; he would distil his grace into my words, and they'd have the effect he wanted on those who would truly welcome them. I'd have much to suffer as a result of my reluctance to put pen to paper and hand certain messages to those who were a source of humiliation to me.

Father Claude insisted that I should never resist this influence from above—no matter what pain or humiliation I might have to endure—but say quite simply what I'd be inspired to say. If I wrote it down, I was to give my Superior the paper, and then take my cue from her. (I kept to this advice, but it lowered me greatly in the eyes of those around me.) He also ordered me to write down my spiritual experiences. I loathed the idea—I used to write out of obedience and then, persuading myself that I had at least done what I was told, I'd burn it; this brought me a lot of suffering. Eventually, I was led to have second-thoughts on my conduct, and forbidden to keep up that pretence any longer.

CHAPTER XIII

IN CALVARY'S MOULD

ONE day, the God of sacrifice asked me to make a will leaving everything to him. I'd already made over to him verbally all my future actions and sufferings, as well as all the prayers that would be offered for me during my lifetime or after my death; but now he wanted it in writing. I was to ask my Superior, he said, if she'd be willing to draw up this document; and he undertook to make it well worth her while. If she declined, I was to approach his servant, Father de la Colombière; however, she fell in with the proposal.

Jesus, my only Love, evinced great satisfaction when I offered him the completed will. He intended using it for his own purposes, he told me, and for the benefit of souls he had in mind. He meant his sacred Heart to be my sole possession, now that he had stripped me of everything else, and he had the deed of gift ready. I had to take it down in my blood to his dictation; the signature was the holy Name of Jesus, which I scratched on my breast with a penknife.[1] Now that I was no longer entitled to anything which might come my way, he would take it on himself to reward to the full anyone who was good to me, as though they'd done it to him personally; as for my Superior, he was going to reward her with a crown similar to St Clare of Montefalco's—he'd add to her merits his own infinite ones, because of her love for his sacred Heart. This made me very happy, for I was really fond of her . . .

[1] 31 December 1678.

she never stinted the supply of food my soul craved—those delicious dishes of humiliation and mortification which my royal Master found so palatable. I'd have liked everyone to lend a hand here, and so give him a real treat. Still, I was never short of this sort of nourishment, God's grace saw to that; my life was one long round of physical suffering, due not only to frequent bouts of sickness and constant weakness, but to other things as well. I was also suffering spiritually—I felt lonely, forsaken, and I could see God being offended; I was persecuted, thwarted and humiliated by those around me; I was tempted by the devil, who never left me alone, but did all he could to torment me; and then there was myself—the worst adversary I've ever had, and the most difficult to get the better of. Added to all this, I was kept busy by as much manual work as I could possibly cope with. But all the while God, in his goodness, never failed to support me.

Not the least of my sufferings at that time was the impression I had that the others just couldn't stand the sight of me. I imagined they must have been finding it extremely hard to put up with me, for it was as much as I could do to put up with myself. This was a constant thorn to me in community, and my only way out was to love my self-abasement. There were plenty of opportunities, too . . . every least thing I did was a source of fresh humiliation—the way they looked at it, I was only the visionary infatuated with her fads and fancies! Any hope of finding some relief or comfort in it all was out of the question; my royal Master had put his foot down there—he wanted me to suffer everything in silence and adopt as my motto:

> ' Suffering I'll meet without complaint,
> Love 'gainst all fear ensures restraint.'

He meant me to leave everything to him. The only relief he'd let me find, if ever I happened to look for a little encouragement, was further anguish and fresh grief. I've always considered this one of God's greatest graces. There was another: in spite of the poor use I've always made of the precious cross, so that I don't deserve it, he has never snatched it away from me. I'd willingly have quite spent myself for my Redeemer in loving recognition and gratitude.

These feelings, and the delights which the cross brought me, had me saying: ' What return shall I make to the Lord for all the wonderful things he has given me? My God, you are so good to provide a place for me at table with your saints, and a share in the spiritual food you offered them! No stint, here, of those delightful dishes prepared for your favourite and truest friends—yes, even for me, a worthless wretched sinner! ' But then, you must appreciate that I couldn't live, or endure this lengthy exile of mine, if I hadn't the Blessed Sacrament and the cross. I've never wished for any curtailment of my sufferings in this vale of tears. The severer my bodily aches, the keener my spiritual joys and the greater freedom of soul I had for thinking of Jesus in his sufferings, and for seeking union with him. More than anything else, I yearned to become a true copy, a perfect reproduction, of Jesus crucified. So I was overjoyed when my good Master set a crowd of hands to work, turning out a finished product good enough for him.

Undeserving victim though I was, my royal Lord never stood aloof from me—he knew my weakness only too well, my incapacity when it comes to doing any good. He'd say to me sometimes: ' I am paying you great respect, my dear child, in availing myself of such noble instruments for crucifying you. My eternal Father handed me over to pitiless executioners for crucifixion, but I am turning you over to people devoted and consecrated to me. I have left you in their power; you are to offer me, for their salvation, all the sufferings they will cause you.' I did so with all my heart, anxious at all times to take upon myself any punishment due to them for their treatment of me—though I couldn't really see that they were guilty of any injustice in furnishing me with sufferings, as I deserved far more than came my way. Of course I get quite a thrill, I admit, in writing about suffering and the happiness it brings. I do believe I could fill whole volumes on the subject, without ever feeling I'd had enough; it's the kind of thing which I do take a pride in writing.*

Once, my royal Master hinted that he'd like to take me aside into a place of solitude—not in a desert, after his own example, but in his sacred Heart. There, he intended giving me the privilege of his most intimate companionship, one dear friend with another; there, he'd give me fresh instructions as to what he wanted of me, strengthening me anew to put them into practice and to go on fighting bravely until death—for I'd still have to meet the onslaughts of many powerful enemies. For that reason, he was asking me to fast for fifty days on bread and water, in honour of the fasting he had done in the desert. I was prevented from doing this by obedience—they were afraid of singularity on my part—and so he indicated that he'd be just as pleased if I spent fifty days without drinking, in honour of his sufferings in that respect on the cross as well as the intensity of his never-ending thirst for the salvation of sinners. This penance I was allowed to do. It seemed very much harder to me than the first one—you see, I've always suffered from such dreadful thirsts, I've often had to take huge cupfuls of water to quench them.

All that time, I had to put up with violent assaults from the devil, and despair was the spearhead of his attack. A creature as wicked as myself, he pointed out, shouldn't aspire to a place in heaven; even now I had no place in God's heart, and I'd be completely cut off from him for all eternity! This made me shed floods of tears. Another time, his attack centred on vainglory. Next, he tried the loathsome temptation to gluttony . . . he'd make me feel frightfully hungry; and then, during my spiritual exercises, he'd call up visions of the tastiest dishes—a source of exquisite agony. My hunger would last until it was time for collation; but as soon as I set foot inside the refectory, a sudden feeling of nausea would come over me, and I'd have to make tremendous efforts to eat anything at all; then I'd no sooner leave the table than back would come my hunger more terrible than before. I made no secret of all this—there was always that gnawing fear of self-deception—and my Superior[1] ordered me to go to her whenever I felt ravenous, and ask for permission to eat. I had to use the utmost force to bring myself to do this, I felt so ashamed; but then, instead of sending me to the refectory, she'd make my visit an excuse for a severe mortification and humiliation—I was to swallow my hunger, would be her comment, and wait until everyone else went to the refectory! I'd suffer in peace after that.

I wasn't allowed to finish my drinking fast that time; but they let me start it again as a result of my prompt obedience when they stopped me. (I spent the fifty days without a single drink —a practice I've followed every Friday.) It was all the same to me whether I was granted or refused the permissions I asked; as long as I could be obedient, that was all I wanted.

[1] Mother Péronne Rosalie Greyfié, who belonged to the first Monastery at Annecy, and was Superior at Paray from 1678 to 1684.

CHAPTER XIV

THE GREAT REVELATION

M Y diabolical persecutions never slackened. Satan tempted me to everything except impurity—my divine Master had forbidden him that entry. Yet, even there, he once caused me frightful misery. It was like this. . . . My Superior happened to say to me: 'Go along and substitute yourself for the King of France[1] in front of the Blessed Sacrament.' While I was kneeling there, I went through such severe and disgusting temptations against purity that I almost believed I was in hell. It went on for hours, this agony, until at last my Superior broke the spell by telling me I could stop representing the King, and impersonate a good Visitation nun instead. Immediately, my trials were at an end. A torrent of consolations surged over me as my royal Master gave me the following instructions. . . . He wanted my life to be one long sacrifice, and so he was going to increase my sensitivity and intensify my queasiness to such an extent that every single thing I did would cause me stress and strain. In this way, even the most trivial and unimportant things would furnish me with opportunities of self-conquest. (I can vouch for the fact of this having been my constant experience ever since.) The only sweetness I should ever know in this world, he went on to add, would be found in the bitterness of Calvary, nowhere else; all the things that normally go to make up pleasure, enjoyment or happiness in this world would, for me, turn out to be ordeals akin to martyrdom.

[1] Louis XIV. His reign, from 1643 to 1715, may be divided into two periods: libertinism and devotion—though this natural division should not be exaggerated.

The way things worked out, this has cut me to the quick, and no mistake; whatever could be described as pleasurable became a torment to me—even the little amusements we are sometimes given. I had to do what the others did—our Lord insisted on that—but the worst of fevers couldn't have been more painful. 'Good Jesus!' I was forced to exclaim, 'pleasure sells dearly when I go a-shopping!' So much misery awaited me at table or in bed, the mere proximity of them reduced me to tears. But my daily duties were what I found altogether unbearable, and visits to the parlour. I don't remember ever going to the parlour willingly; I was always sore put to it to overcome my reluctance, even to the point of falling on my knees to God for strength to conquer myself. Writing was no less of a trial; it wasn't merely that I used to do it on my knees —there were those other reasons! It hurt me when people treated me with respect, said nice things about me, or gave me a pat on the back; the most ambitious of social climbers would have felt being humiliated, scorned and passed over far less keenly. 'My God!' I used to burst out, 'unleash all hell's fury against me rather than the empty praise, flattery or approval of human tongues! I'd sooner meet the onrush of humiliations, distress, set-backs and shame!' My thirst for these things was insatiable, and it was all his doing; but he made so sure that they'd be keenly felt, I couldn't stop myself from betraying it now and then. . . . To think that I couldn't suffer without it showing! To think that I was so unmortified, so far from being the least bit humble! It was unbearable. My one consolation lay in the fact that I could resort to loving my self-abasement. I'd thank my royal Master, then, for letting me be seen for what I really was, so that I'd count for nothing in human eyes.

In addition to all that, he meant me to welcome everything as coming from him. I wasn't to go after things myself; I wasn't to make any plans, but leave everything to him. I was to be just as grateful to him for suffering as for pleasure. When things were most trying and humiliating I was to reflect that

I deserved it all, and more besides; the misery I suffered—I was to offer it for the people who were distressing me. I was always to speak of our Lord with great reverence, of my neighbour kindly and with admiration, and never of myself—or at most a passing reference of no consequence, unless he ordered me to do otherwise for his greater glory. Anything good or meritorious I was always to attribute to him, everything evil to myself. For consolation I was to turn only to him, and to nothing or nobody else: and even if he offered me any, I was to make him the sacrifice of giving it all back. I was to have no care for anything—completely destitute and detached. I was to love him alone—everything else in him or for his love. In all things I was to see Jesus only, and what concerns his glory, in utter forgetfulness of self.

Although love for our Lord was to be the motive of everything I did, he intended each of my activities to have some special reference to his divine Heart. At recreation, for example: the anguish, humiliations, mortifications and the like, which he'd take care I never lacked—I was to accept them gladly so as to have something special to give him. It was the same in the refectory: he wanted me to forego the nicest things as my tribute to him—this was to be the theme of all my actions. He went on to forbid me ever to judge, accuse or condemn anyone but myself. There were lots of other things he taught me; I was astonished at the number of them. However, he told me I hadn't anything to be afraid of—he was a good Master, his wisdom as a teacher and director only surpassed by his power in getting things done. I can vouch for the truth of that. . . . Willy-nilly, in spite of my natural reluctance, he had me doing what he wanted.

One day, kneeling before the Blessed Sacrament during the octave of Corpus Christi,[1] I was deluged with God's loving favours. Inspired to make some return, and to give him love for love, I heard him say: 'Do what I've already so often asked you; you can't show your love in a finer way than that!'

[1] June 1675.

He disclosed his divine Heart as he spoke: 'There it is, that Heart so deeply in love with men, it spared no means of proof —wearing itself out until it was utterly spent! This meets with scant appreciation from most of them; all I get back is ingratitude—witness their irreverence, their sacrileges, their coldness and contempt for me in this Sacrament of Love. What hurts me most is that hearts dedicated to my service behave in this way. That is why I am asking you to have the Friday after the octave of Corpus Christi set apart as a special feast in honour of my Heart—a day on which to receive me in holy Communion and make a solemn act of reparation for the indignities I have received in the Blessed Sacrament while exposed on the altars of the world. I promise you, too, that I shall open my Heart to all who honour me in this way, and who get others to do the same; they will feel in all its fulness the power of my love.'

When I told him I didn't know how to fulfil this long-expressed wish of his, he told me to apply to Father de la Colombière whom he had sent me for that purpose. I did so; and the good Father ordered me to put in writing (for God's greater glory) everything I'd told him concerning the Sacred Heart of Jesus, together with several other related matters. He was most encouraging, this saintly man—God was not only showing me, through him, how to fit in with his plans, but also reassuring me against my dreadful fears of being deceived, which were a constant trial. It was a great blow when our Lord removed him from this town to work for the conversion of heretics[1]—he had been such a help in the short time he spent here; but I bowed wholeheartedly to God's will. Later, when I ventured to reflect on what this loss really meant to me, our Lord took me to task at once: 'What's this! I am your beginning and your end; isn't that enough for you?' There was nothing I could do after that but leave it all to him. I was sure he'd take care to see I had everything I'd need.

[1] Fr de la Colombière left Paray in 1676 and was sent to England as chaplain and preacher to Her Royal Highness the Duchess of York, Marie Beatrix d'Este, at the court of St James. Cf. Appendix III.

So far, I had found no way of fostering devotion to the Sacred Heart, which was all I lived for. Here's how God gave me my first chance. . . . While I happened to be in charge of the novitiate, the feast of St Margaret fell on a Friday.[1] I asked the novices if, instead of paying me the little compliments they'd planned for my feast day, they would pay them to the Sacred Heart of our Lord Jesus Christ. They did their best to humour me, and made a tiny altar; above it they put a piece of paper on which was sketched a little pen-and-ink portrait of the Sacred Heart. In front of this shrine we tried to give our Lord such homage as he inspired us to make. The result was that I incurred a good deal of humiliation, opposition and mortification—and the novices too! I was accused of wanting to introduce a new devotion.

For myself, these sufferings were a great comfort; the only thing I dreaded was that the divine Heart would be brought into disrepute—the comments I heard around me struck like swords at my breast. I was forbidden to display any more pictures of the Sacred Heart; a few private devotions—that was the most they would allow.[2] In my distress, I could think of no one to turn to, except our Lord himself. He became the prop for my dejected spirits, repeating all the time: 'Don't be afraid; I shall reign in spite of my enemies, in spite of all opposition.' This cheered me up immensely—his reign was all I wanted—and I just went on suffering in silence, leaving him to see to the defence of his cause. Persecutions of every sort continued to be my lot, so that it seemed as though all hell were let loose against me, everything geared to my destruction. I must admit, however, that I never enjoyed such inner peace, nor felt so happy, as when they threatened me with prison and planned to arraign me—like my good Master—before an earthly prince,[3] as a victim of ridicule, a visionary infatuated with the offspring of her imagination.

[1] 20 July 1685.
[2] Mother Mary Christine Melin was now Superior; she ruled from 1684 to 1690.
[3] Emmanuel Theodore de la Tour d'Auvergne, Cardinal de Bouillon. This Prince, a Cardinal at 24, and commendatory Abbot of Cluny, was then living in Paray. He was shortly to champion Fénélon against Bossuet.

G

I'm not saying this to make you think I suffered a lot; I'm really trying to set on record God's great mercies to me. What I valued, and clung to more than anything, was the share he let me have in his cross. A delicious treat—that's how I found it; and it has never palled.

CHAPTER XV

REPARATION—
A PAINFUL RETREAT

HAD I been allowed to go often to Communion, then I'd have achieved my heart's desire. As I was dreaming longingly of this one day, my arms full of sweepings, my divine Master appeared to me. ' My child,' he said, ' I've noticed your sighs; I'm so delighted with your heartfelt longings that, if I hadn't already instituted the Sacrament of my Love, I'd institute it now for you—to give myself the pleasure of making my home in your heart, your soul the cradle of my love.' These words imbued me with such passionate fervour, and my soul knew such transports of joy, I could only stutter: ' Love! God's prodigal love for so wretched a creature! ' An incentive—that's what this incident has been to me all my life—to spur me on to return that unselfish love.

Another time, as I was praying before the Blessed Sacrament one Corpus Christi Day, a blazing human form was suddenly set in front of me—the heat from it so intense, I thought I was on fire too. I understood that I was looking at a soul from purgatory, and its pitiful state made me weep. He told me, this soul, that he was a Benedictine monk who had once heard my confession; he'd urged me, on that occasion, to go to holy Communion—and now, as a reward, God was letting him appeal to me for help in relieving his sufferings. He asked me to do and suffer everything I could for the next three months, and make it over to him. I promised—after I'd asked my Superior's permission—and then he told me the reason for his bitter sufferings. . . . He'd preferred his own interests on earth to God's glory, too keen on his own reputation; then there was his lack of charity towards his brethren; finally, his love for creatures had been too natural, and he'd shown it unwisely in his spiritual dealings with them—to God's great displeasure.

I'd find it very hard to put into words what I had to suffer during those three months. That poor soul never left my side, and whichever part of me was nearest to him seemed all on fire; the agony was so intense, I was practically in tears the whole time. My Superior, moved with pity, laid down some pretty good penances for me, in which the discipline figured prominently. The outward suffering she caused me, in her charity, greatly soothed these inner torments of mine—the tiny sample, which the holiness of God's love was giving me, of what those poor souls have to suffer. When the three months were up, you wouldn't have recognised my visitor: bathed in bliss and glory, he was standing on the threshold of eternal happiness. He assured me, as he thanked me, that he'd act as my patron before the throne of God. The last few months had made me ill; but as my sufferings came to an end with his, I was soon well again.

My royal Master gave me to understand that, whenever he felt like washing his hands of any souls he wanted me to suffer for, he'd treat me like a damned soul, letting me experience the loneliness that comes over it at the hour of death. I've never met with anything so terrible—there just aren't any words to describe it.

Once, when I was working by myself, I was shown a nun —a nun who was still alive. 'Look here, now!' I distinctly heard a voice saying. 'Here's a nun who is a religious in name only. My Heart is just about sick of her and on the point of leaving her to herself.' It was a moment of such awful terror, I fell flat on my face. I stayed like that for some time, I simply couldn't move. I volunteered to suffer whatever God's justice demanded, as long as he wouldn't forsake this soul. It seemed then as though God's justice was being turned against me—nothing but frightful agony and loneliness, and a crushing weight on my shoulders. If I looked up, I'd see an angry God equipped with rods and scourges preparing to descend upon me. If I looked down, hell appeared open at my feet to swallow me up. Rebellion and confusion reigned inside me. I was all beset with violent temptations, particularly to despair. I ran everywhere to escape from God's pursuit, but there was nowhere I could hide; I'd have suffered anything to have avoided his gaze. I was frightfully ashamed—I imagined that it was obvious to everyone what I was going through. I couldn't even pray or explain my difficulties; I could only sob: 'What a fearful thing it is to fall into the hands of a living God!' At other times, face downwards, I'd say: 'Strike, my God! Cut, burn and destroy everything which offends you; spare neither body, life, flesh nor blood of mine . . . but save that soul!' I couldn't have put up with such a painful state for long, I must admit, without the support of our Lord's loving mercy under the severity of his justice. As it was, I fell ill; and recovery was difficult.

Painful circumstances of that kind were not infrequent; and once, when he had shown me the punishments he meant to inflict on some souls, I threw myself at his sacred feet, saying: 'Vent all your anger on me, my Saviour; better blot me out from the book of life than damn these souls you bought so dearly!'

'But they don't love you!' was his answer. 'They never stop making life difficult for you.'

'That doesn't matter,' I replied; 'as long as they love you, I shall go on asking you to forgive them.'

'Don't interfere,' he said; 'I can't put up with them any longer.'

'No, Lord!' I cried, holding him tighter. 'I shan't let you go until you've forgiven them.'

'Willingly,' he agreed, 'if you will be surety for them.'

'Of course, my God,' I answered; 'but you'll always be paid in your own coin—from the treasury of your sacred Heart!' . . . an arrangement that met with his approval.

Another time, while picking hemp—a work we did in common—I retreated into a tiny courtyard close to the Blessed Sacrament. Working there on my knees, I suddenly felt utterly recollected in soul and body. Then I saw the Heart of Jesus, so lovable, so worthy of adoration, outshining the sun. It appeared to be the centre of flames of love, and all around were Seraphim singing in wondrous harmony:

> 'Love's triumphant, love delights,
> Love his sacred Heart excites!'

They invited me to join them, these blessed spirits, in their praises of that divine Heart, but I didn't dare. They reprimanded me for this, however, and told me that that's why they were there—to join with me in paying an unending homage of love, adoration and praise. They were going to take my place in front of the Blessed Sacrament, they added, so that—thanks to them—I could love him uninterruptedly; in the same way, too, they were to have a share in my love, suffering through me as I rejoiced through them. They drew up the deed of partnership there and then, inscribing it on the Sacred Heart with letters of gold in the indelible handwriting of love. The effects of this vision, which lasted from two to three hours, have remained with me all my life; not only has it been a great help, but it is a constant source of delight. Acutely embarrassed though I feel, I have always—since that day—called these spirits 'partners' when I pray to them. That grace made me so anxious to achieve absolute purity of intention, and gave me such a tremendous appreciation of the purity needed if we would talk with God, that I used to feel anything but pure.

Then there was the time one of the sisters[1] was in a coma.
. . . There seemed to be no hope of her being in a fit state
to receive the last sacraments—a great worry to the Community,
especially our Mother,[2] who told me to promise our Lord that
I'd do anything he'd ask of me, to win the sister that grace.
I'd no sooner obeyed than my royal Master promised me that
the invalid wouldn't die before she could receive the blessings
we were quite justified in wanting her to have . . . as long
as I promised him three things—things he was asking of me
unconditionally: the first, never to refuse any office in religion;
the second, on no account to refuse to go to the parlour; and
the third, to write whatever I was asked. The whole of me
shuddered at this request, so great was my reluctance, my
distaste for all that. 'Dear Lord,' I replied, 'you certainly
know how to cajole me! Very well, I'll ask permission.' My
Superior gave it at once, even though I made no attempt to
hide the agonies I'd go through. Our Lord insisted on my
making the promise in the form of a vow, so that I shouldn't
be able to go back on it any more. But, oh dear!—what a lot
of times I've let him down! He might, at least, have put an
end to the distaste I felt; but no, it's lasted all my life. Still,
the sister did receive the sacraments.

To show just how unfaithful I could be, amid all these
tremendous favours, I'm going to mention the time I decided
to have a second attempt at inscribing the holy Name of Jesus
on my breast.[3] I was terribly keen to go into retreat and
thought that this would be a fine means of preparing for it, a
few days beforehand. The way I did it, however, left me with
several sores. The day before the retreat began, I told my
Superior about them; she thought I ought to have some treatment for my injuries, in case they made me seriously ill. This
had me complaining to our Lord: 'Jesus, my only Love, are

---

[1] A member of the ' Little Habit ', just a child. Her name was Antoinette Rosalie
de Sennecé, and she had made a vow of chastity at the age of 7. She was only 13
when she died on 26 April 1684, after conditionally pronouncing her religious vows.
[2] Mother Greyfié; cf. note p. 74.
[3] This was in the autumn of 1679.

you going to let others see what I've done to myself for love of you? Is it really beyond you—the chief antidote for all my ills—to make me better? ' Touched, at length, by my distress at having to reveal what I'd done, he promised me that the following day would find me cured. He was as good as his word. Our Mother, however, sent me a little note—I hadn't been able to catch her to tell her about my cure—with instructions to let the sister[1] who brought the message look at my sores . . . she'd do something for them. But now that I was cured, I decided, I was excused from doing what was in the note, while I looked for our Mother to tell her the news.

Oh dear, this delay of mine in obeying met with such severity! Our Mother was not alone in this . . . there was my royal Master; for something like five days he trampled me underfoot, and all I could do was bewail my disobedience —non-stop in my penances to crave his pardon. As for my Superior—acting under our Lord's influence, she'd no mercy for me this time. She stopped me going to holy Communion— the worst punishment possible for me in this life; I'd a thousand times rather have been condemned to death. Not only that, but she made me show my sores to the sister after all—who wouldn't touch them, now that they were better. I was made to feel acutely embarrassed, all the same; but then, I'd displeased my royal Master, so such things were of little account; in my sorrow, I'd have suffered any kind of torment. Eventually, when he had shown me his dislike of the tiniest lack of obedience in a religious and let me taste the penalty of it, our Lord came in person—the last days of my retreat— to dry my tears and restore my spiritual vitality.

Yet, for all his loving kindness, there was no end to my grief. I'd only to remember displeasing him, and I'd burst into tears. He really brought home to me the importance of obedi- ence in a religious—I hadn't quite grasped it before, I must admit . . . but this would take too long to explain. As a

---

[1] Sister Marie Madeleine des Ecures.

punishment for my fault, he told me, all trace of the holy Name which it had cost me so much pain to carve on myself (in memory of what he suffered in taking it) would vanish, and so would my earlier efforts—the marks of which were still evident in various ways. My retreat was a painful one, I can tell you!

CHAPTER XVI

CONFORMED TO THE CRUCIFIED

ONE long round of sickness—that was my lot; I was never well for four days at a time. One morning,[1] when I was very ill, my voice almost inaudible, our Mother came to me with a note—I was to carry out its instructions, she told me. She needed reassuring, the note informed me, that it was God's influence at work in me and responsible for all I was going through. If this were so, she wanted him to give me five months of perfect health, during which I'd need no treatment of any kind. If, on the other hand, some diabolical influence or my own temperament were responsible, then there was to be no change. I can't tell you how pained I was at receiving this note—its contents were no secret to me, even before I read it! I was told to get out of the infirmary, and our Lord saw to it that their words and tone of voice were of the most hurtful and mortifying sort.

Well, I delivered the note to my royal Master—aware as he already was of what it contained—and he gave me this reply: 'You have my word for it, child—as a proof that you are not being led astray, I'd give you five years of perfect health, never mind five months; or any other guarantee she'd care to ask!'
. . . It happened at Mass, at the elevation: I had a vivid sensation of all trace of sickness lifting; it was like a dress being pulled over my head and hung up on its hook. Now I felt as strong and healthy as one of those hardy individuals

---

[1] 21 December 1682.

who can't remember a day in bed. But the specified time passed,[1] and then I was back as I was before.

Once, when I was running a high temperature, my Superior made me leave the infirmary to go into retreat.[2] It was my turn, you see; and she told me: 'Off you go, I'm entrusting you to the care of our Lord Jesus Christ. It's for him to guide, rule and cure you, as he wills.' Although a bit surprised —after all, I was shivering and feverish—I went off happily to do as I was told, glad to be utterly dependent on my good Master and to have a chance of suffering for love of him. Painful or pleasant?—whichever kind of retreat he had in store, I didn't mind. 'It's all grist to the mill,' I found myself saying: 'as long as he is pleased and I love him, that's all I want.'

I was no sooner alone, my retreat begun, than he appeared. Lovingly he lifted me from the floor, where I was lying shivering with cold and pain. 'There, now!' he said; 'at last you're entirely mine, completely in my hands. Sick, that's how they've given you to me; so I'm going to send you back to them quite well again.' He gave me such a clean bill of health, you'd have thought I'd never been ill. They couldn't believe their eyes, my Superior especially—she knew all the circumstances.

I've never known such joys and delights in a retreat. It was one uninterrupted stream of graces, of intimate endearments from Jesus Christ my Lord, his holy Mother, my guardian angel, and my saintly father Francis de Sales; I really thought I was in heaven. I'm not going to make a list of all these unusual graces here; it would take too long. But this I will say: my kind Director deigned to leave the imprint of his holy Name on my heart and seal it outwardly with the engraving tool of love. This was to give me ever so much joy and consolation, greater in its intensity than any pain or distress

---

[1] 21 December 1682 to 21 December 1683. When the five months were up, Mother Greyfié had told Margaret Mary to ask that her good health be prolonged until one full year from her first request.
[2] In the autumn of 1681.

my way could have done. He wanted to console me, you see, for the grief I felt when he'd wiped all trace of his Name from my breast.

There was only one thing missing—the cross. I couldn't live without it nor could I enjoy any pleasure, even though it were heavenly and God-given. To see myself conformed to Jesus in his sufferings—that was my sole delight; and so my one thought was to be as hard on myself physically as obedience left me free to be. I really put my body through it, to be sure; I stopped at nothing, not even food or sleep. I'd made myself a bed from bits of broken pots, and I used to lie down on this quite happily; my whole frame would quiver and shudder, but I took no notice. There was one particular penance I was really set on; its very harshness was an added attraction for me. Here was a way of making myself suffer, I thought, in reparation for the insults our Lord meets with in the Blessed Sacrament. (And it was not only deliberately disrespectful souls I had in mind, but also my own wretched sinful self.) I was on the point of suiting action to idea, when my royal Master stopped me. He meant to send me back to my Superior in good health, he reminded me; after all, she'd left me in his care. If I were to make a sacrifice now, and give up doing what I'd planned—that would be much more to his liking. God, being a spirit, looks for spiritual sacrifices. Dutifully, I did no more about it—that was quite enough for me!

As I went up to make my Communion, one day, the sacred Host seemed as dazzling as the sun—I couldn't stand the glare—and there in the centre was our Lord, holding a crown of thorns. Shortly after I'd received him, he put the crown on my head. 'Take this crown, my child,' I heard him say, 'as a token of the one that will soon be yours, to make you more like me.' I couldn't grasp what he meant, at the time; but I knew all about it soon enough. I felt two terrible blows on my head, and ever since I've always had the impression that the crown of my head is encircled with sharp, painful thorns; I'll feel them puncturing my skin to my dying day. No limit, now, to my gratitude! Great graces—that's what God gives to his tiny victim; but alas, as I've often told him, victims should be innocent; and here am I, a criminal. I must admit, however, that I feel more indebted to my royal Master for this costly crown than if he had made me a present of all the diadems of earth's greatest sovereigns. Nobody can take this one away from me, that's the point. Besides, it brings me the good fortune of often having to lie awake at night, and so gives me an opportunity of talking to Jesus, my only Love. My good Master couldn't lean his head against the cross, and neither can I bear to lay mine on a pillow. This was a source of unheard-of joys and encouragement, as I found myself taking ever so slightly after him. He meant me to join the merits of this pain of mine to his own crowning with thorns and, through them, to ask God the Father for the grace of conversion for sinners and humility for those whose intellectual pride was so hurtful and offensive to him.

On another occasion, during carnival time (about five weeks, that is to say, before Ash Wednesday),[1] our Lord appeared to me after holy Communion carrying his cross; he was a mass of wounds and bruises, his precious blood flowing freely. ' Will no one take pity on me? ' he asked, his voice saddened with pain. ' Will no one have the sympathy to share my sufferings in the pitiful state to which sinners reduce me, especially at times like these? ' Tearfully and sorrowfully I threw myself at his sacred feet as a volunteer, my shoulders bent to the heavy load of that nail-studded cross. The sensation of its crushing weight was the beginning, for me, of a deeper awareness of the gravity and malice of sin, for which I had such a heartfelt loathing, I'd far rather have thrown myself into hell than commit one deliberately. ' Horrible sin! ' I used to think. ' What a loathsome way to treat so good a God! '

---

[1] Carnival, in the old days, began on Twelfth Night (6 January) and lasted till midnight of Shrove Tuesday. About the time of St Margaret Mary, the public festivities of carnival were gradually being restricted, due to papal influence, to the six or seven days immediately preceding Ash Wednesday.

He showed me that just to carry the cross wasn't enough—I'd need to fasten myself to it, if I were to be his faithful companion and share the pain, scorn, shame and other outrages which he endured. I surrendered myself, at once, to whatever he had in mind for me; I let myself be fastened to the cross, just as he liked . . . and it was by a sickness which soon had me feeling the sharp points of the nails with which that cross was studded—acute pains, with nothing but scorn and humiliations for sympathy . . . one long train of what was most naturally distressing. The pity of it is, no suffering could match the extent of my guilt; this fact has kept me ever sunk in shame since the day God let me see the hideous appearance of a soul in mortal sin, and the gravity and malice involved in setting self against the infinitely attractive goodness of God. That vision is the source of my keenest sufferings. I'd cheerfully have started out by suffering the full penalty due to my sins, if—in so doing—I could have prevented myself committing them; anything rather than be so contemptible—even given the guarantee that God, in his infinite mercy, would forgive me and forget the punishment.

The attraction suffering held for me, which I've just been describing, generally lasted the whole of carnival time. By Ash Wednesday I used to feel my end had come; there was never any comfort in relief—that only made things worse. But then, all of a sudden, I'd find I had enough strength and energy to manage the Lenten fast. My royal Master has always, mercifully, let me do that—though sometimes I'd be so prostrate with pain, I'd start a particular practice with the feeling that I'd never be able to finish it. Then, with that behind me, I'd have the same difficulty with another. 'O God,' I'd pray, 'give me the grace of keeping on to the end!' I was grateful to my royal Master, all the same, for measuring my moments by the clock of his passion, striking the hours on the chimes of his sufferings.

Whenever he intended to bestow a new cross on me, he used to prepare me for it by untold endearments and such tremendous spiritual delights, I couldn't have endured them permanently. 'My only Love,' I'd cry, on such occasions, 'take back all these delights as a sacrifice. Keep them for saintly souls who will use them to give you greater glory than I can. You are all I want—and the nakedness of Calvary, where I can love you for yourself alone. Strip me of everything else, so that my love for you may be unalloyed—free from personal advantage or gratification!'

Now and then, at times like these, he'd delight in doing just the opposite—the wisdom and experience of the Director prescribing happiness when I'd have liked suffering. Still, joy and pain both come from him, and are—like all his benefits—purely products of his pity. He has never had to deal with anyone as difficult as me, so frequently disloyal and always so very fearful of being misled. I've been amazed, hundreds of times, that so much reluctance on my part never drove him to destroy me, to let me sink; yet, no matter how serious my faults, my good Jesus, true to his word, never deprives me of his divine presence. But if ever I do anything to displease him, he makes that presence so disturbing, I'd prefer any kind of torture—willingly undergo it time and again rather than, stained with sin, endure God's presence or be within sight of his holiness. I tried desperately to hide, to get right way; but it was useless. No matter where I fled, I'd find him there—such frightful torture, devoid of all relief and affording no heart to look for any, I'd think I was in purgatory. I'd cry out, sometimes, in my agony: 'What a fearful thing it is to fall into the hands of the living God!' That was how he cleansed my stains, if ever I was slow or careless about penalising myself.

God, in his goodness, never gave me one of his special graces without first of all making me suffer tortures of that kind. I'd feel as though I'd been thrown into purgatory, where I was drowning in humiliations and shame, and where I had to suffer more than words can tell. Yet, all the time, I knew an enduring peace. Nothing, I felt, could ever disturb that peace of soul—frequently agitated though my soul was, in its lower part, by my own passions or by my diabolical adversary. The devil tried his level best; distressed and restless souls afford him the easiest prey* . . .[1]

---

[1] The MS, in the Saint's own handwriting, ends here. Fr Rolin, S.J., who had asked her to write it, left Paray in the autumn of 1686. As she was given no further instructions, St Margaret Mary stopped writing; four years later she died—17 October 1690.

APPENDIX I

CHRONOLOGY

22 July 1647	Birth of Margaret Mary.
25 July 1647	Baptism in the parish church of Vesrovres.
c. 1651	She made her vow of chastity.
1655	Her father died, aged 41.
Summer 1656	Her first Communion at Charolles.
1657-61	Sickness.
25 May 1671	Her first visit to Paray.
20 June 1671	She enters as a postulant.
25 August 1671	Clothed in the habit (Mother Hersant Superior).
2 June 1672	Mother de Saumaise elected Superior.
6 November 1672	Margaret Mary was professed.
27 December 1673	First revelation of the Sacred Heart.
1674	Second and third revelations.
February 1675	Bl Claude de la Colombière arrives at Paray.
June 1675	Final revelation of the Sacred Heart.
August 1676	Bl Claude de la Colombière leaves Paray for England.
21 May 1678	Mother Greyfié elected Superior.
13 May 1684	Mother Melin elected Superior, and Margaret Mary assistant.
1 January 1685	Margaret Mary appointed Novice-mistress.
20 July 1685	First public devotion to the Sacred Heart in the novitiate; criticisms of the community.

21 June 1686	First public devotion to the Sacred Heart by the community at the instigation of Sister des Ecures.
1 January 1687	Margaret Mary relinquished post of Novice-mistress.
May 1687	Re-elected as assistant.
17 October 1690	Death of Margaret Mary.
18 October 1690	She was buried beneath the nun's choir.
18 September,1864	Beatified by Pope Pius IX.
13 May 1920	Canonised by Pope Benedict XV.

APPENDIX II

THE PROMISES OF THE SACRED HEART
EXTRACTS FROM LETTERS

To Mother de Saumaise, at Dijon.[1]   *24 August 1685.*

Quite frankly, dearest Mother, the crushing weight of my sufferings seems to paralyse me; I'm hardly the same person any longer, and no good for anything. There's only one thing I can do, one privilege left to me, and that's to talk about our Lord's sacred Heart. I'm going to give you a tiny peep into some of the special favours which I believe[2] I've had from him—undeserving as I am.

He has brought home to me afresh the delight he takes in being honoured by his creatures, and I thought I heard him make me the following promises . . . No one who has a deep devotion to the Sacred Heart will ever lose his soul. Since all blessings come from our Lord, they will be lavished especially on those places where an image of the Sacred Heart is displayed to win him love and honour. In this way, he will mend broken homes, help and safeguard families in time of need. Communities, where this image is honoured, will be permeated with the soothing influence of his love; and he will dispel the threat of God's just anger by restoring them to his

---

[1] Mgr Gauthey, *op. cit.*, II, letter xxxv, pp. 296-297.
[2] St Margaret Mary frequently uses such phrases as ' I believe ', ' I thought ', ' It seemed as though ', ' If I'm not mistaken ', when describing her visions—due not to uncertainty of the facts, but to her constant fear of being deluded. She had also been told to write in this way by Mother Greyfié, so that she might not become too firmly attached to her own opinions and unable to give them up at the judgment of her superiors.

favour, if sin has caused them to fall from grace. For the first person who will do him the kindness of having this image made, he has a special promise—to make him holy and save his soul. . . .

To Mother Greyfié, at Semur.[1]   *1685.*

If only you knew how I feel: the urge impelling me to love our Lord's sacred Heart, an urge that brooks no denial! Life, it seems, is mine just for that—and yet I do quite the contrary. He goes on favouring me all the time; and I show only ingratitude for payment. One recent grace was a visit from him which has done me a great deal of good—to judge by the effects in my soul.

He corroborated my impression of the untold pleasure he takes in being known, loved and honoured by his creatures, by promising me—if I'm not mistaken—that all those who have a true devotion to him and consecrate themselves to his sacred Heart will never lose their souls. He is the source from which all blessings flow—blessings which he will bestow abundantly in every place where the image of his divine Heart is set up and honoured. Families divided by discord he will bring together again; he will also be the shelter and help of any family faced with trouble, and which calls on him with confidence. The soothing atmosphere of his love will permeate every religious community which honours his sacred Heart and places itself under his special protection; for the sake of these communities, he will deflect the force of God's justice— he will restore them to his friendship when they forfeit it. He has given me to understand that his sacred Heart is the holy of holies, the sanctuary of love. He wants the world to recognise him now as the mediator between God and men. Unlimited in power, he can give the world peace—averting the punishments which our sins bring on us, and winning mercy.

---

1 Mgr Gauthey, *op. cit.*, II, letter xxxvi, pp. 299-300.

To Mother de Saumaise, at Dijon.[1]   *May 1688.*

Although the Heart of our good Master lets me find comfort in receiving your letters and sending you mine, still he doesn't leave me free to do so as often as I'd like. That's why I'm seizing the opportunity of a few spare moments to open my heart to you and give you my idea of devotion to the Sacred Heart. It's what you said you wanted, but it's something I find very difficult to do, because—wayward and worthless though I am—I seem to be utterly lost in that divine Heart. Its depths—unless I'm very much mistaken—are past all fathoming, and there he discloses to me the treasures of his love: the graces reserved for those who consecrate themselves to him and, by their sacrifices, win him all the honour, love and glory they possibly can.

One Friday, during holy Communion, this unworthy slave of his—if she's not mistaken—heard these words: ' I promise you, out of the prodigal pity of my Heart, that my all-powerful love will grant to those who receive holy Communion on nine consecutive first Fridays of the month the grace of final perseverance, so that they shall not die in my disfavour without the sacraments. My divine Heart will be their sure refuge at the last.' In addition, he promised his unworthy slave that, if she concentrated on loving him to the exclusion of everything else, he would himself speak to his Father on behalf of all those who may recommend themselves to her prayers.

How should I ever tell you, Mother, the story of the Sacred Heart's mercies to me? Never were they greater or more prodigal, despite my thanklessness. An obstacle to the extension of his glory and the flow of his grace to souls—that's how I see myself; and this is due to the lax life I lead, for which God is often justly enraged with me. . . .

[1] Mgr Gauthey, *op. cit.*, II, letter lxxxvi, pp. 395-399.

To her Director.[1]   *1689* (?)

It's quite beyond me to set on record the whole story of this lovely devotion as I know it. I've no way of disclosing to all the world the treasures of grace stored in the Sacred Heart of Jesus. What can I do to reveal his purpose—the prodigal out-pouring of grace on those who practise this devotion! I entreat you, reverend Father: leave no means untried of instilling it in every heart. In ways beyond question, Jesus has shown me that he means to establish this important devotion everywhere, and so recruit untold loyal servants, perfect friends and truly grateful children—all this, chiefly through the Fathers of the Society of Jesus.

The Sacred Heart is a treasure-house of graces and blessings past all counting. I know of no other devotion in the whole range of the spiritual life which affords the same guarantee of lifting souls in a very short time to the peak of perfection and allowing them to relish the sweetness of serving Jesus Christ. Indeed, I'd even make it a principle: given the knowledge that our Lord finds this such a welcome devotion, there isn't a single Christian—striking merely the tiniest sparks of love— who wouldn't begin it immediately.

Do your very utmost to get religious to adopt it. They will find it so helpful, they won't need to look any further for ways of reviving their first fervour, or of restoring lax com-munities to strict observance, or of bringing the most exemp-lary religious to the very summit of perfection.

My divine Master has informed me that those who labour for the salvation of souls will acquire the art of touching the hardest hearts, and see their work crowned with success, if they have a tender devotion to the Sacred Heart and use their influence to encourage and establish it everywhere.

Lay people, too, will find in this devotion all the help they

[1] The exact recipient of this letter is unknown. Certainly it was not Fr Colombière, but it could possibly have been Fr Rolin or Fr Croiset. Cf. Mgr Gauthey, *op. cit.*, II, letter cxli, pp. 626-628.

need: peace in their families, rest amid their toils, the blessing of heaven on all their ventures, comfort in time of trouble. There, in the Sacred Heart, they will find a home and shelter all their life long—but, above all, at the hour of death. A lifetime of tender and true devotion to the sacred Heart of our Saviour and our Judge ensures the blessing of a happy death!

Lastly, it's quite evident that there's no one in the whole wide world but would receive every help from heaven in all circumstances, provided he has a truly grateful love for Jesus —the essence of devotion to the Sacred Heart.

APPENDIX III

BLESSED CLAUDE DE LA COLOMBIÈRE

CLAUDE DE LA COLOMBIÈRE was born at St Symphorien d'Ozon, midway between Vienne and Lyons, on 2 February 1641. His family came of noble Burgundian stock and his father was a public notary, Claude being the third of six children.

He was educated at the College of the Holy Trinity at Lyons, which was staffed by the Jesuits. Here, he made his first Communion. Here, he was confirmed by the saintly Cardinal Archbishop of Lyons, Alphonse Louis de Plessis de Richelieu. And here, at the age of seventeen, he took part in a literary entertainment for Louis XIV, who visited the College in 1658 on his way through Lyons.

On leaving school, Claude joined the Jesuits—though he had to overcome his father's opposition first—and entered the Novitiate at Avignon on 22 October 1659, where he spent two years of probation. In 1662 he returned to the College at Lyons to pursue his studies for the priesthood. He also taught at the College and, for three years, held the chair of Rhetoric at the University. He was ordained in 1671, and entered his tertianship (third year of probation) in 1673. Towards the end of 1674 he was appointed Superior of the Jesuit house at Paray-le-Monial, when he was only thirty-four years of age.

During the following year he came to know St Margaret Mary in the Visitation convent there, and was given by her a message from our Lord urging him to spread devotion to the Sacred Heart. He consecrated himself to this work on 24 June 1675—the Friday after the octave of Corpus Christi!

After only eighteen months in Paray, he was sent to England as chaplain to Princess Mary Beatrice of Modena who had recently married the Duke of York, brother of Charles II. She had wanted to be a nun, but Pope Clement X suggested that she could serve God better in those troubled religious times by marrying the Catholic heir to the English throne. She came to live in St James's Palace, off Piccadilly, which Henry VIII had built on the site of an old leper hospital dedicated to St James. Mary Tudor had died in the Palace; Charles II and his brother, James, were born there.

One of the conditions of her marriage was that she should have a private chaplain. The first was an indiscreet French Jesuit, who compromised his position and had to return to France. Fr Colombière took his place and arrived at the Palace on 13 October 1676. Here, in the Queen's Chapel, he said Mass and preached; and so it was the Catholics of London who first heard devotion to the Sacred Heart publicly advo- cated. His conversations with the King paved the way for the deathbed reconciliation of Charles II by Fr Huddleston, a Benedictine monk.

Two years after Fr Colombière's arrival in England, the Papist Terror broke out in 1678. He was imprisoned on sus- picion of treason, but no evidence could be found. He spent three weeks in prison and was then deported to France. When he arrived in Lyons, he was suffering from tuberculosis con- tracted in the English gaol. During the autumn of 1680, he was allowed home to stay with his brother at St Symphorien. Eventually, in 1681, the doctors suggested that the mild clean air of Paray would suit him better, and there he spent his last days. He died on 15 February 1682, at the age of forty-one; he had been a Jesuit for twenty-two years.

The accession of James II made Mary Beatrice Queen of England in 1685, but she had to flee the country in 1688. She never forgot Fr Colombière, nor the devotion to the Sacred Heart he taught her, and was the first of the royalty of Europe to beg the Pope to institute the feast for which our Lord had asked St Margaret Mary.

Claude de la Colombière was beatified by Pope Pius XI on 16 June 1929.

NOTES

p. 3.

From contemporary evidence it seems that this incident must have taken place in her godmother's private chapel at Corcheval, and not in the parish church at Vesrovres. Madame de Fautrières occasionally invited Margaret to spend a few days with her; Corcheval was only three miles from Hautecour, the Alacoque home. The chapel still exists on the edge of the terrace bordering what had once been a medieval fortress. When the chapel was restored in 1920, a statue of the little saint at prayer was placed in the porch.

p. 4.

This convent at Charolles belonged to the Poor Clares. The nuns followed a less austere rule than the one first given to St Clare and her nuns at S Damiano, and the enclosure laws were relaxed. This was due to Pope Urban IV, and so this branch of the Poor Clares came to be known as Urbanists.

p. 5.

After the death of Madame Alacoque's husband, a new lease of the property was drawn up in her brother-in-law's name. This individual, Toussaint Delaroche, was an excellent and efficient farmer. He despised the better-educated Madame Alacoque, who came from a cultured, well-to-do, legal family. As agent for the estate and guardian of the children, he considered himself master of the place, and Margaret's mother was not the type of character to assert herself.

p. 9.

' Sans que personne s'en affligeât, ni mît en peine que moi, qui ne savais où recourir, ni à qui m'addresser, sinon à mon asile ordinaire, la très Sainte Vierge, et mon souverain Maître, à qui *seul je pouvais découvrir* les angoisses où j'étais continuelle-ment plongée.'

The words in italics are supplied from a contemporary copy, as the MS is torn at this point.

p. 19.

' Il me semblait alors que mes liens étaient rompus, et que je n'avais plus rien à craindre, pensant que quand la vie religieuse serait une *espèce de purgatoire* il me serait plus doux de m'y purifier le reste de ma vie, que de me voir précipitée dans l'enfer.'

The words in italics are missing from the MS.

p. 25.

Why St Hyacinth? Could it have been because Hyacinth (accepted into the Dominicans by St Dominic himself) was, by dispensation, professed after only six months' novitiate and immediately made a superior? After all, Margaret Mary was anxious to waste no time! Fr G. Tickell, S.J. (*Life of Bl Margaret Mary*, 1874, p. 47) suggested that it was because St Hyacinth also had difficulties to surmount in following his vocation; but I have been unable to find proof of these difficulties.

p. 25.

' Mon frère étant donc de retour, me dit: " On veut quatre mille *livres*, c'est à vous de faire ce qu'il vous plaire de votre bien, car la chose n'est pas encore arrêtée." '

The word in italics is not in the MS. It is difficult to give in modern terms the sum demanded for the dowry. Apart from the vast difference in monetary values between now and then, the value of the *livre* (no longer in use) varied from one part of France to another. My suggestion of £600 is only a very rough-and-ready equivalent; the actual sum may possibly have been greater.

p. 29.

' Je la regardais, et ma Supérieure aussi, comme mon Jésus-Christ en terre.'

' Mère Thouvant's father had been one of the two founders of the Visitation convent at Paray-le-Monial in 1626 and she had been one of the first to take the veil there. She had been sixteen when St Jeanne Françoise de Chantal, on one of her visits, had laid her hand in blessing on the young novice's head, with the injunction that her fervour must be restrained, lest it injure her health, for " by her virtue and good judgment she would render valuable service to the convent " (Bougaud). She had been four times superior and was now assistant to Mère Hersant as well as novice-mistress and had been professed forty-four years. Mère Hersant had entered the Visitation convent in the Rue St Antoine, Paris, where she had often seen St Jeanne Françoise de Chantal and had been for twenty years directed by St Vincent de Paul. She and her assistant had brought the convent to a high state of order and piety. The two chief devotions were to the Passion and the Blessed Sacrament. The thirty-four choir Sisters counted among their members daughters of most of the noble families of Burgundy. One was Marie de Fautrières-Corcheval, daughter of Margaret's godmother. There were also six lay Sisters, and six oblates or associates.'—*These Three Hearts*, Margaret Yeo, 1940, pp. 166-7.

p. 47.

Here we have the divine origin of the devotion known as the Holy Hour, which is essentially an act of reparation. An Archconfraternity was established in Paray, at the Visitation Monastery, and hundreds of thousands of associates are listed in its registers. In 1946 it had 150 affiliated Confraternities in all parts of the world.

p. 48.

'. . . que le médecin connut qu'il avait fort longtemps que je la portais : et elle me dura encore plus de soixante accès.'

p. 57.

'Il me reprit si fortement là-dessus, qu'une fois, voulant nettoyer le vomissement d'une malade, je ne pus me défendre de le faire avec ma langue et le manger.'

I felt it was necessary to tone down the effect of the original here, in the interests of English readers of the present day.

p. 58.

' " Tu connais donc bien que *tu ne peux rien* sans moi " '

A tear in the MS had made it necessary to take the words in italics from a contemporary source.

p. 58.

'Et une fois que j'avais fait quelque soulèvement de coeur en servant une malade qui avait la dysenterie, il m'en reprit si fortement, que je me vis contrainte, pour réparer cette faute, en portant verser ce qu'elle avait fait, d'y tremper ma langue un long espace de temps et d'en remplir ma bouche; et l'aurais avalé, s'il ne m'avait mis alors l'obéissance devant les yeux, laquelle ne me permettait pas de rien manger sans congé.'

A paraphrase seemed preferable to omitting the passage.

p. 66.

'Mais je ne lui voulus faire aucune ouverture de coeur pour cette fois; et comme il vit que je me voulais retirer, crainte *d'incommoder la* Communauté, il me dit si j'agréerais qu'il me vînt *voir* une autre *fois,* pour me parler dans ce même lieu.'

The words in italics are either missing or indecipherable in the MS.

p. 73.

' Mais j'avoue que je me délecte si fort en parlant du bonheur de souffrir, qu'il me semble que j'en écrirais des volumes entiers, sans pouvoir contenter mon désir; et mon amour-propre se satisfait beaucoup en ces sortes de discours.'

p. 94.

At this point, another hand, contemporary with St Margaret Mary, has added the following words: ' en fait son jouet et la rend incapable d'aucun bien '—' he makes them his playthings and turns them into good-for-nothings.'